D0577987

ECHOES OF THE WHISTLE

ECHOES *of the* WHISTLE

An Illustrated History of the Union Steamship Company

GERALD RUSHTON

. . .

Introduction by Leonard G. McCann

Douglas & McIntyre

VANCOUVER

COPYRIGHT © 1980 BY GERALD A. RUSHTON

All rights reserved. No part of this book may be reproduced or transmitted in
any form by any means without permission in writing from the publisher,
except by a reviewer, who may quote brief passages in a review.

Douglas & McIntyre Ltd.
1615 Venables Street
Vancouver, British Columbia

■   ■   ■

Canadian Cataloguing in Publication Data

Rushton, Gerald A., 1898–
    Echoes of the whistle

    Sequel to the author's Whistle up the inlet.
    ISBN 0-88894-286-9

    1. Union Steamship Company of British
Columbia – History.   I. Title.
HE945.U25R882   387.506'0711   C80-091223-3

■   ■   ■

Design by Nancy Legue
Typography by George Payerle
Printed and bound in Canada by D.W. Friesen & Sons Ltd.

To the memory of Margaret, who gave me the title Whistle Up the Inlet *for my 1974 book, as well as the title for this illustrated sequel. When voyaging aboard Union ships, she often saw poetry in the life of British Columbia's coast people. For my sake, Margaret sacrificed innumerable outdoor weekends while I was preoccupied over many seasons with the Union's unforgettable summer excursions. Her inspiration and help were invaluable to my completion of the Union Steamship story.*

Contents

Introduction

In 1889, just three years after the founding of the City of Vancouver, a small group of citizens who wanted to move around Burrard Inlet with a little more celerity than the transportation of the day provided and who saw as well the need for a coastal shipping line, established, with the aid of some outside capital, the Union Steamship Company. Within three years the company was serving northern ports and within ten it was shipping men and materials to the Klondike Gold Rush. But between the Port of Vancouver and the Alaska peninsula lies the whole of the British Columbia coastline, a maze of twisting inlets, bays, and fjords where pioneering settlers were establishing logging, mining, and fishing communities. It was to these ports of call that the Union Steamship Company carried the means for survival and growth. Later, the company also established resorts where holidayers and residents from the Lower Mainland could enjoy a break from their workaday routine, sailing there on a Union ship. The company provided excursions for a day or overnight or longer, some ships running cruises to the north.

It was the familiar little red-and-black-funnelled ships of the Union fleet that pioneered development of the British Columbia coast. They served, for nearly three-quarters of a century, over 200 communities, ranging from tiny industrial float camps to large, bustling holiday resorts. This fleet of coastal messengers, whose masters threaded their way through little-known and half-surveyed inlets and channels with incredible skill and seeming nonchalance, chalked up a safety record unsurpassed by any equivalent service anywhere in the world. Not surprisingly then, nearly a third of the early Pacific coast pilots had served their apprenticeship as Union Steamship masters.

When the company ceased operations in January 1959, it was more than just the closing of a local service: it was the passing of a pioneer era. A link with Vancouver's beginnings was severed and what had been an integral part of coastal life suddenly became history—the record of the past.

In *Whistle Up the Inlet* Gerald Rushton told the story of the company's operations from an inside point of view. Here, in the companion volume, *Echoes of the Whistle,* the emphasis is on the visual record, which is very largely that of the ships themselves.

The people of Vancouver and of British Columbia have been wonderfully served with this photographic record of a notable part of their maritime heritage.

—Leonard G. McCann
Curator, Vancouver Maritime Museum
August 1980

Preface

I feel most fortunate in having this opportunity to fulfil the demand for a sequel to my *Whistle Up the Inlet,* which brought me a flood of nostalgic reminiscences from coast pioneers afar and near.

Some of their vivid recollections of the Union Steamship Company's imprint on the history of the British Columbia coast, and on the lives of its early settlers, are reflected in this photographic record of the company's ships and those who manned them. Undoubtedly, many more such memories will spring to life in the viewing of these rarely seen historic pictures. For here, in print for the first time, is a treasury of every ship that flew or served under the Union flag. Illustrated also are historic artifacts that will enliven even the most dormant of memories.

In preparing this second volume of the Union Steamship story, I relied largely on personal notes preserved over the years, and on company records to which I had full access in my official capacities. I had seen to it—though not without a little artifice—that my work was partly divided between the Union office and the outside operations. It was this continuing contact with the marine side, coupled with my fascination from the early 1920s with the coast and old-timers' stories, that impressed on me a sense of historical significance that otherwise could not have been acquired.

Echoes of the Whistle, however, also reflects the generous contributions of several individuals. I am especially indebted to Leonard G. McCann, curator of the Vancouver Maritime Museum, for his assiduous research in unearthing historic artifacts relating to the pioneer Union vessels, and in locating several elusive photographs of ships. He further assisted me in the verification of some records. Michael Duncan, director of the Vancouver Maritime Museum, also gave his considerate support.

The Vancouver City Archives accorded me the privilege of using their reference facilities. In compiling the meanings and derivations of Indian and Spanish ship names, I obtained valued information from the Vancouver Maritime Museum, courtesy of Dr. Robert D. Levine, associate curator of linguistics, B.C. Provincial Museum. I also thank the staff of the Vancouver Public Library's history department for helping me greatly in this research.

Constance and Mary Darling graciously made available to me the papers of their father, Henry Darling, and provided a photograph of their grandfather, John Darling.

I am grateful to my Union colleague, Harold N. Crompton, for the use of *Chilcotin* brochures and a selection of snapshots; to A.J. "Budge" Jukes for the use of his photographs of the Union-Tidewater division's vessels.

Due acknowledgement is made to the following sources: Lewis & Dryden's *Marine History of the Pacific Northwest* (1895 edition); Walbran's *British Columbia Coast Names;* Ruth Greene's *Personality Ships of British Columbia;* and Irene Howard's *Bowen Island.*

I regret that it was not possible to include in the text the names of many more Union Steamship men who contributed so greatly to the company's wide range of services. I well know that they too performed—far beyond the line of normal duty—many unsung acts of friendship for the people of the coast settlements. Memories of such kindness are also echoes of the Union Steamship tradition that cannot be stilled by the passage of time.

Map of Ports of Call

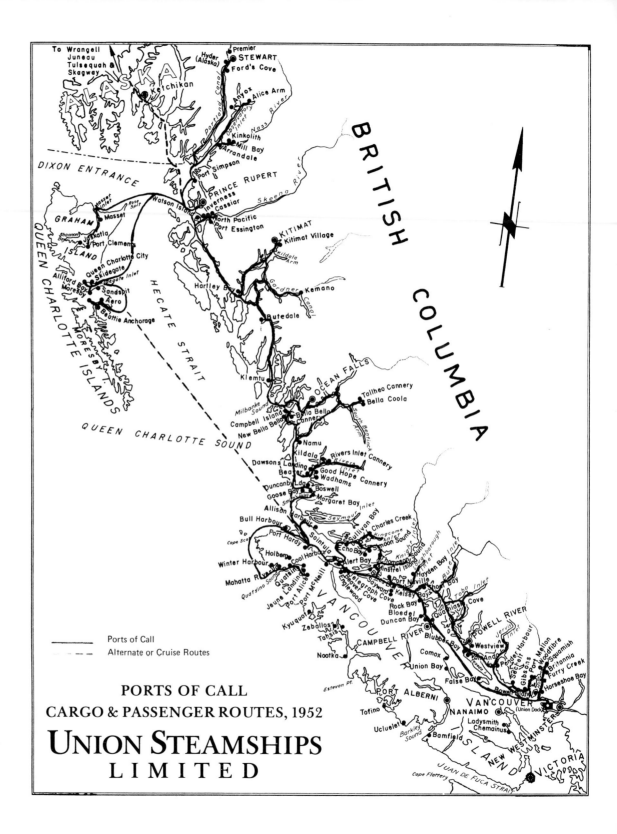

Ports of Call
Alternate or Cruise Routes

PORTS OF CALL
CARGO & PASSENGER ROUTES, 1952
UNION STEAMSHIPS
LIMITED

1889-1918

The First Red-and-Black-Funnelled Ships

Among the islands of the Inside Passage,
deep in inlets where sheer cliffs disappear into
waters of mysterious depths, where distant
snow-capped peaks breed roaring creeks
and lacy waterfalls—in that country the
whistle of a little Union steamer was a song.

It brought out wives whose house and garden
were floating on giant logs, it brought
miners down to shaky wharfs and kids out of
school.

It was Boat Day, a big day.

—Torchy Anderson

The Union Steamship Company of British Columbia
Limited was incorporated on 1 July 1889, "to acquire, carry
on and extend the business known as the Burrard Inlet Ferry
Company, as a going concern, and to own steam ships,
lighters and vessels, for mail, passenger and freight traffic,
in the waters of British Columbia, or elsewhere." The Union
was the first line to use Vancouver as its home port. The new
port, in the almost landlocked Burrard Inlet, was the last big
harbourage to come alive in the Puget Sound and Strait of
Georgia areas of the Pacific northwest. The population of
Vancouver (renamed from Granville), was barely 1,000 when
the city was incorporated on 6 April 1886; by 1891, four years
after the arrival of the Canadian Pacific's first transcontinental
train, the population had increased to 14,000.

Until the Union's handy and staunch vessels appeared on
the scene, there was no convenient and frequent transport
along the northwest coast. Vancouver's pioneer merchants
had difficulty getting supplies to the new logging camps and
settlements north of Vancouver and lumbermen had the same
problem transporting work crews to their campsites.

The floating equipment taken over by the Union comprised
three steam tugs and eight scows, with an assessed value of
$20,000. Two smaller tugs, the *Leonora* and the *Senator,* had
been bought in 1886 by Capt. Donald McPhaiden, of the
Burrard Inlet Ferry Company, from Capt. James Van Bramer,
a pioneer mariner in Burrard Inlet. The *Senator* was employed
as a ferry, making four or five trips daily from Moodyville
(later a part of North Vancouver district) across to Vancouver
in charge of Capt. Hugh Stalker, who handled the Union's
first mail contract. Vancouver's mails then came from New
Westminster by stage to the upper end of Burrard Inlet,
thence by a small boat to Moodyville. Ferry passage cost 10
cents each way, livestock 50 cents, and often a barge was
towed carrying horses, cattle, and machinery. McPhaiden had
bought the 76.0' *Skidegate* in 1889 for harbour towing and to
service upcoast contracts.

John Darling—a director and former general
superintendent of the Union Steamship Company of New
Zealand who had crossed Canada in 1888 in the company of
William Van Horne of the Canadian Pacific Railway—
provided the inspiration and experience for organizing a
Vancouver-based coastal line. On a visit to Vancouver,
Darling learned from leading businessmen and mariners
(including Capt. William Webster who chanced to be one of
his former shipmasters) of the serious lack of transport to
upcoast points, and the primitive navigating conditions.
Having some idea of the railway's expansion plans for its
"terminal city," Darling saw the opportunity for a local
steamship line with vessels that could maintain continuous
service in all kinds of weather between Vancouver and the

upcoast settlements. After initiating steps with a city group to found a company, Darling went to Britain to raise capital from Scottish shipping interests for a fleet-building program. The overseas shareholders were given representation on the board of directors.

At the first meeting of the new company in 1890, seven permanent directors were elected and the new company was capitalized at $500,000 in shares of $5 each. Colonel Hamersley, a London barrister who had practised in New Zealand (and there introduced rugby football) before bringing his family to Vancouver, was the Union Steamship Company's first chairman. Because of John Darling's association with the famous New Zealand Union line, the name was adopted and its funnel colours of red and black chosen.

Darling raised enough capital to buy three small steel ships, whose hulls were to be prefabricated in sections by Bow McLachlan & Company at Paisley, Scotland, and brought round The Horn to Vancouver for assembly.

In April 1890 the company bought the old city wharf from the City of Vancouver for $10,000. The Union directors took it for granted that they now owned it, as did the city fathers, since the wharf site was shown on the Granville townsite plan of 1870. It therefore came as a shock when the CPR claimed that under their charter from the Dominion government they held the rights to the foreshore on which the wharf had been built. The ownership issue was not pressed until March 1899, when the CPR's solicitors insisted upon recognition of their foreshore rights.

This complex legal point would have taxed the judgement of a Solomon. The area marked on the Granville plan, before Confederation, had been "dedicated to the public as a townsite" by the Colonial government, and the Union's case was supported by the mayor of Vancouver. The CPR,

however, contended that the British North America Act granted the Crown, in the name of the Dominion government, that part of the foreshore used for harbour purposes prior to Confederation. It was argued that the rights had never left the Crown when it disposed of the property to the CPR.

After an earlier CPR writ to recover the property was withdrawn, the Union commenced suit for ownership in 1902. The case dragged on until the CPR offered a compromise, giving the Union a permanent lease of the premises for a nominal rent, and access across the tracks, upon the Union's acceptance of the CPR's claim. This friendly agreement was reached upon the advice of the Union's counsel, E.V. Bodwell. To my knowledge, the company never collected its $10,000 from the city, but it did enjoy the wharf site rent-free for 12 years, and then occupied it for more than half a century for a minimal fee.

Over the next eight months the pioneer yard in Coal Harbour contributed greatly to both the history of Vancouver and the marine development of the Pacific northwest coast. It was important to the young city's payroll, since about 100 men, even professional men and qualified mariners, were employed as shipwrights, mechanics, and day labourers. Darling's assistant at the site was James Frith, later a chief engineer of the company, who had apprenticed to A. Stephen & Sons of Govan. A key helper was Jimmy Bogart, who was to spend a lifetime as boss carpenter at the Union dock workshop. Another was Alfred (Andy) Wallace from a boat building family, who went on to found his own shipyard in 1894 on False Creek. Others who helped were Capt. John Gosse, Cory Wood (later MP for Alberni), and Capt. John Macpherson.

While the new vessels were being built in Britain Captain Webster, the managing director, went to India and purchased the 180.0′ steam yacht *Cutch,* which had been built for the Maharajah of Cutch. After hiring a crew, he steamed her over 10,000 miles via Singapore, the China Sea, and Japan to Vancouver.

The arrival of the *Cutch* on 3 June 1890 drew crowds to the Union wharf at the foot of Carrall Street. After a refitting, she was scheduled to service upcoast settlements, but was first contracted out to the Canadian Pacific Railway, which urgently needed a vessel to make daily sailings to Nanaimo with passengers and rail freight in order to link CPR's transcontinental express with Vancouver Island. The *Cutch* connected at Nanaimo with the Esquimalt & Nanaimo Railway line to Victoria, recrossing the Gulf of Georgia the following day at 7 A.M. on weekdays. However, she was free for the Union's business on weekends, and was booked for summer excursions and picnics on Howe Sound, and for pioneer outings to Bowen Island and to Gibson's Landing (now Gibson's), as well as for cruises to Mayne Island, Ladner's Landing (now Ladner), Pender Harbour, the Fraser River, and Victoria.

To increase tonnage capacity, the company partly rebuilt the *Skidegate,* installing new Bow McLachlan engines and boilers and enlarging the main cabin, before restoring her to service in April 1891. With increased speed, she could occasionally relieve the *Cutch.* For several years the *Cutch* drew increasing local patronage, and railway business also increased on the Nanaimo ferry connection.

The iron steamer *Grandholm,* 243.0′ and 1,361 gross tonnage, was chartered in May 1891 to carry the hull sections, engines, and boilers of the prefab ships, filling almost all her space at Glasgow. On 19 August she completed a fast voyage to Vancouver in 83 days. Her cargo was loaded onto scows and towed to a shipyard site in Coal Harbour leased from the CPR: a narrow stretch of property running east from high water at the foot of today's Gilford Street at Georgia. A yard office and blacksmith's shop were built, along with two shipways for laying down, assembling, and launching the new ships. The land had to be levelled and cleared by cutting back the forest, since there was only a trail beyond what is now Cardero Street. The project was directed by Darling's son Henry, who had just returned from Montreal with his Scottish bride.

The keel of the passenger vessel *Comox* was laid within two weeks of the unloading of her steel sections, and she was launched six weeks later on Saturday afternoon, 24 October 1891.

In April 1892 the *Comox* became the pioneer logging-camp ship, providing a scheduled service with mail, passengers, and freight. The weekly route included calls at Gibson's Landing, the Sechelt Indian wharf, Welcome Pass, Van Anda, Comox on Vancouver Island, Lund, Manson's Landing on Cortez Island, Read Island, Stuart Island, thence to Loughborough Inlet and Port Neville via Sayward's Camp.

The *Capilano* followed the *Comox* down the ways on 5 December 1891. She was a bigger ship, primarily a freighter, and was quickly engaged in contracts, one of which was to carry sandstone south to build the city's new post office.

The last of the famous Union trio to be launched at Coal Harbour, in April 1892, was the *Coquitlam,* a freighter similar to the *Capilano.* Before the ship's outfitting was complete, she was already engaged for an unusual charter by the Victoria-based Sealers' Association. Although the charter presented an element of danger, the Union's management welcomed it as an opportune and lucrative contract. Her assignment was to deliver supplies to the Victoria sealing schooners in the Gulf of Alaska, then return south with the sealskins.

The *Coquitlam*'s engagement was far more dangerous than the management had realized and involved her in a costly incident which became a serious international issue.

There was an unresolved dispute over sealing rights in the North Pacific, and the United States was watchful of any encroachment on its Alaskan territorial rights. Capt. E.E. McLellan, master for this voyage, had been instructed to make all transfers with the sealers "on the high seas," but after completing some transfers outside United States waters, he was forced to put into Port Etches, Alaska, for repairs. There officers of the U.S. revenue fleet boarded and arrested the *Coquitlam* on 22 June 1892, along with her cargo of 6,000 sealskins. She was ordered to steam into Sitka and was held there for several months until an American court declared her a "prize" on a charge of illegally transferring cargo inside U.S. waters. She was then escorted to Port Townsend, Washington, where the sealskins, valued at $90,000, were confiscated. The Victoria sealers' agent on board, Capt. William Grant, claimed that the seizure was a premeditated act.

Canadian newspapers carried caustic editorials on the seizure, one charging that it was "part of a deliberate plan to cripple the [sealing] fleet for the season." Protests reached the governor general in Ottawa, and went from there to Lord Salisbury in London. But it was not until 1897 that the U.S. Circuit Court of Appeals reversed the Sitka judgement, ruling that the seizure had been illegal. Meanwhile, the *Coquitlam* had been released to the Union on the surrender of bonds to the value of $600,000. These were now returned to the company.

In 1921, 24 years after the reversal of the Sitka judgement, an arbitrary compensation settlement of $48,000 was made with the Union by the United States—barely half of the company's claim for loss of operating revenue and general damages.

Almost simultaneously with the loss suffered over the sealing misadventure the company suffered another financial setback. Captain Webster had entered into a contract with the Canadian Pacific to run a feeder service with freight and passengers between Portland and Victoria, or Vancouver, to link the CP's projected fortnightly service to the Orient with the new White Empresses. Under the impression that he was assured against loss, Webster entered into the agreement by engaging the deep-sea vessel *Tai Chow* and, after September 1891, by using the *Grandholm* as a replacement. The latter ship had been retained by the Union for a short period after delivering the prefab ships. Because of a competitive service by the Upton line from Portland to the Orient via Victoria, Webster's connecting shuttles proved unprofitable. The Union withdrew service after a crippling loss of more than $30,000, partly incurred for expenses that had not been detailed in the charter. The Union board, being in no financial position to take the matter to court, accepted a settlement of only $15,000.

The double blow from the seizure of the *Coquitlam* and the heavy deficit on the Portland ferry operation placed the young company close to bankruptcy and forced the negotiation of a large loan with the Bank of British Columbia, the Union fleet and entire plant being mortgaged as security. However, the success of the *Comox* logging-camp route in 1892–93 restored confidence that the financial difficulties could be overcome by cutting overhead and avoiding outside ventures. In October 1892 an annual subsidy of $60,000 was granted by the Dominion government for mail and year-round service to the northern communities and logging camps, as the postal and immigration departments were concerned that service be maintained along the northwest coast of the province.

Nevertheless, the company's finances remained critical for three years. Captain Webster went to Britain to explain the losses to the overseas shareholders and to get more capital subscribed. Although his mission was successful, he resigned office shortly after his return and Capt. Donald McPhaiden took over as manager for a brief period.

The company suffered another blow on 12 November 1892 when the *Cutch* and the E & N Railway steamer *Joan* collided in Nanaimo's harbour entrance, but with no loss of life or serious damage. Admittedly, the *Cutch* had been in competitive pursuit of Capt. William Rogers's new *City of Nanaimo,* which had the backing of the Dunsmuir coal interests and was a serious competitor on the Gulf of Georgia run. Despite some interference by the *Joan,* the *Cutch* was held in default by Chief Justice Sir Matthew Begbie, whose stern rulings stopped further racing rivalry between the pioneer coastal steamers.

Alfred Hamersley, who had presided over the company's formative years, retired as chairman in 1893, but retained a seat on the board until 1896. He was prominent in the real estate boom on the north shore of Burrard Inlet until he returned to Oxfordshire in 1905 where he won a seat in the British Parliament, and in 1916 raised and led an artillery regiment to France.

Gordon Tyson Legg, agent of the United Trust & Edinburgh Mortgage Company, who had joined the Union's board in 1892, became the new chairman. He tried every way to increase revenue, even renting out part of the wharf shed in winter. The *Capilano* and the *Coquitlam* were used for a spell in a season's halibut fishing. The tug *Leonora* carried loads of stone to pave Vancouver's streets. The *Comox* made two sailings weekly, with one trip through Seymour Narrows to Rock Bay. Calls were added, by settlers' requests, at Quathiaski Cove and Heriot Bay, and on certain trips into Phillips Arm and Bute Inlet.

In 1894, Henry Darling became the Union's manager. After completing the shipyard project in Coal Harbour, he had served as superintendent engineer, and as secretary of the Union line. As well as being manager, he continued to supervise maintenance of the ships and all construction work.

An improvement in general trade followed through 1894, and chairman Gordon Legg reported a gross profit of $12,000 to the overseas shareholders. Despite this progress, the Bank of British Columbia was ready to sell off the ships to retire a first mortgage of $12,000; however, the Bank of Montreal, on the security of personal notes from Legg and a partner, took over the Union Steamship debt. It was later assumed by the local stockholders in the form of 6 per cent debentures, marking a turning point in the affairs of the company.

In 1895 the *Capilano* secured a contract to haul stone south for the new parliament building in Victoria, and another for towing booms to the Brunette sawmills. Through 1895–96, more passage berths were needed on the logging routes, and in early 1897 the upper deck of the *Comox* was closed in amidships to provide 12 more staterooms. Under her first master, Capt. Charles Moody, she was popular with settlers and loggers alike. With their support she drove off two competitors, including a vessel owned by Canadian Pacific Navigation Company. In this type of trade the Union line had no peers. By this time the *Cutch* had been withdrawn from the Nanaimo route and laid up, partly because of the lack of covered accommodations and cabins. An unexpected event brought her back into service in an entirely new role.

On 24 May 1897, the *Coquitlam* sailed north on the first scheduled fortnightly service to the canneries. Her route included calls in Rivers Inlet, on the Skeena River, and at

Metlakahtla, Port Simpson, and two canneries on the Nass River. Accommodation for 50 passengers had been provided and gave the company more flexibility. The *Skidegate* was retired from service and her Bow McLachlan engines used in the building of the *Chehalis,* a new service tug.

In late June and early July of 1897 came reliable news of rich gold strikes centred near the confluence of the Yukon River and its Klondike tributary. It confirmed year-long rumours that had trickled through from the north and from mining brokers in Seattle. In Seattle, Victoria, and Vancouver the news triggered the Klondike Gold Rush as fortune-hunters from around the world sought transportation to the goldfields. Shipping houses arranged to get men and supplies to Skagway, the nearest port from which to reach the goldfields overland.

Vessels loaded with men and stores were already leaving Seattle for Skagway, the steamer *Alki* sailing on 18 July with more than 100 prospectors. The Canadian Pacific Navigation Company placed its crack steamer *Islander* on the Alaska run leaving Victoria on 28 July. The Union's *Capilano* was, however, the first British vessel to sail from a British Columbia port in the Klondike trade. She left the Union wharf on 22 July 1897 on a chartered trip to Dyea in Pyramid Harbour, northwest of Skagway, loaded with horses, cattle, drivers, and passengers. Dyea was the point of debarkation for wagon parties and livestock being driven over the lower Chilkoot Pass. The usual approach to the higher and treacherous White Pass route was from the wide-open boom town of Skagway, where thousands of gold-seekers became stranded before the winter. Henry Darling hastily built livestock stalls, and extra berths and deck bunks for passengers.

Departures from the Union wharf followed at an average of 10-day intervals. It was a popular waterfront pastime to watch a Union ship leaving for Alaska, crowded with would-be miners and their kits, the foredeck piled almost to the bridge with hay and equipment. Many passengers slept in the open. The *Coquitlam*'s accommodations were again increased to take up to 157 passengers.

Meeting the demand of the Alaska-bound traffic was helped by speeding up the remodelling of the *Cutch,* with new engines being installed at a cost of $40,000. More passenger space was enclosed to provide a total of 60 cabin berths, and the addition of deck bunks gave her a licence for 200 passengers. After exceeding 14 knots on trials, the rebuilt *Cutch* sailed for Skagway on 13 June 1898, in command of Capt. Holmes Newcombe. She quickly proved to be the fastest ship in the gold rush trade, setting a record of 88 hours to Skagway that remained unbeaten while she was in service. For more than two years, with only one interruption for a major overhaul, the *Cutch* serviced most of the company's Alaskan business.

The Klondike Gold Rush had peaked by 1900, but nevertheless it was a major loss when near midnight on 24 August the *Cutch* ran hard aground on Horseshoe Reef 25 miles south of Juneau. She was northbound with a full cabin list, and hit foul weather for two days before stranding. Having been on the bridge almost continuously, and for 17 hours on the day of the accident, Captain Newcombe had left the watch in charge of the second officer only 30 minutes before his ship ran off course onto the reef at full speed. Newcombe launched five boats and got everyone ashore and camped, all passengers later being picked up and taken to Juneau. It was believed that the *Cutch* could be salvaged, and for many weeks she showed no signs of breaking up, apart from losing upper-deck housework. However, fearing winter storms, the directors abandoned her to the underwriters against Newcombe's advice. She was recovered by a salvage company and towed to Juneau, and later restored to service as an American ship.

For a brief period the *Coquitlam* took over the Skagway run, but the need for more service on the northern B.C. coast was increasing. The *Capilano* already had been withdrawn from the Alaskan trade and was running regularly to Rivers Inlet and the Skeena River, which now had eight canneries, and to the Nass River. She called at many way ports, such as the Indian settlements at China Hat (Klemtu), Hartley Bay, and the village wharf at Kitimat. She was soon joined by the *Coquitlam* on the northern coast to serve new settlements at Namu and Bella Bella, and farther south at Bute and Knight inlets; Alert Bay, where the early B.C. Packers' cannery was working; Sointula; Hardy Bay, and Bella Coola.

In March 1900, Gordon Legg took over as managing director, but Henry Darling remained as secretary-manager for another 18 months before becoming manager of the British Yukon Navigation Company. The need for a second logging-camp vessel was demonstrated when the busy *Comox* grounded in Frederick Arm, leaving only the *Coquitlam* available to relieve for three weeks. In early 1900, plans were drawn for another passenger vessel with more cargo space to be built at the Wallace shipyard on False Creek, using the stout wooden hull of the former schooner *J.R. McDonald.* This 120.0' ship had more cabins and general facilities than the *Comox.* Her reliable Bow McLachlan engines were shipped from Scotland, and she was launched in False Creek on 28 September 1901, and christened the *Cassiar.* She was to achieve fame along the B.C. coast second only to that of the Hudson's Bay Company's historic *Beaver,* and was accorded a boisterous welcome at all stops on entering the logging-camp trade under Capt. Charles Moody in early 1902.

The logging routes were now extended to cover an area over 200 miles northwest of Vancouver as far as Seymour Inlet. Between them the *Cassiar* and the *Comox* completed four round trips weekly, serving the new settlements and logging camps around Port Hardy and beyond Minstrel Island. They made frequent stops at float landings, besides a number of midstream stops to drop a few boxes of groceries and exchange camp mail bags. Letters were handed in and given a "ship cancellation," then put in the purser's sack. The *Cassiar* was routed weekly to Campbell River, Granite Bay, Rock Bay, and Salmon River. Apart from the main route through Seymour Narrows, the schedules alternated, either traversing the tenuous and intricate passage of Surge Narrows and Okis Hollow into Johnstone Strait or following the inside passage along Lewis Channel through the fiercely tidal Yuclataw Rapids to Shoal Bay and Stuart Island.

After 1900, the company withdrew its Burrard Inlet ferry service, which was taken over by the North Vancouver Ferry & Power Company with the new steam ferry *North Vancouver No. 1.* The Union's *Senator* and *Leonora,* familiar harbour sights for 20 years, were used in towing and charters until they were sold in 1904. Later, the tugs *Coutli* and Chehalis were assigned to special contracts and general towing.

Captains of the early Union ships included some renowned mariners. B.L. (Barney) Johnson was master of the *Comox* and the *Capilano* before 1904. George Gaisford followed Charles Moody on the *Cassiar.* Her later masters included John Cowper, the colourful Jack Edwards who favoured a buccaneer's garb but without shoes, Robert Wilson, John Boden, James Findlay, and John Muir.

The *Cassiar* was adopted as "our own" by the loggers, and this ungainly vessel came to be called The Loggers' Palace. In charting seldom-used channels, of which there were few official charts, her stout wooden hull bounced off many rocks.

Rough sketches of the difficult landings were made in a wheelhouse notebook. In her 1,730 voyages and 750,000 miles of steaming, she had only one major stranding; that one was in Simoon Sound in 1917 and no one was injured. There was much roistering aboard her when the bar was in use, yet her masters kept firm control, aided by the pugilistic skill of husky mates. Often the captain "closed shop" firmly when large camp crews were paid off at shutdowns. Her first pursers were Percy Chick, Bob Bryce, and Charles V. (Trix) Coldwell. Coldwell later became purchasing agent and port steward.

Encouraging revenue from increased trading by the *Coquitlam* and *Capilano* in northern B.C. influenced the Union board in 1904 to plan for a larger passenger steamer in the 200.0' range to serve the northern ports. The Canadian Pacific's *Princess Victoria* and the Boscowitz line's first *Venture*, which sailed out of Victoria, both offered considerably more passenger space in serving the Skeena River canneries. An exciting report had also come from eastern Canada that the Grand Trunk Pacific Railway was considering a transcontinental terminal in northern British Columbia. Another more direct factor that encouraged expansion was confirmation of important gold and silver mining activity in the Portland Canal area.

Accordingly, in April 1904 the Union contracted with Bow McLachlan to lay down the *Camosun*, a powerful steel vessel with excellent cabin accommodations of the Atlantic type, and ample deck space for cannery workers. She had a cargo capacity of 300 tons for southbound loads of canned fish or pulp. The Union's first coast liner sailed from the Clyde on 19 February 1905, through Magellan Strait and up the Pacific coast under Capt. C.B. Smith, but had to undergo deck repairs at San Francisco. This delayed her arrival at Vancouver until 20 June. She was a splendidly finished vessel, with saloons fore and aft on her upper deck and a mahogany-panelled dining saloon.

The *Camosun* left Vancouver on 4 July for her maiden voyage to Port Simpson via Bella Coola, Skeena River, and cannery ports. This was before Prince Rupert was founded, although Union ships stopped when required for a boat landing off Tuck's Inlet, as the uncharted harbour was then called. The *Camosun* played a historic role in the founding of Prince Rupert. Before the city had been laid out, or the harbour even half surveyed, this company announcement appeared in the Vancouver *News-Advertiser* on 18 April 1906:

Union S.S. Co. of B.C. Ltd.

New steel passenger steamer *Camosun* sails from company wharf, Vancouver, after midnight of Wednesday, April 25, for Alert Bay, Rivers Inlet, Port Essington, Prince Rupert, Kaien Island, Port Simpson, Portland Canal, and all points on the northern British Columbia coast.

A news item on 27 April stated: "Up to the present there has not been any more than a general survey of the harbour. . . . This is necessary before the city is built and trade is invited to the place."

Taken together these two items illustrate the Union company's bold enterprise in helping establish coastal communities.

The *Camosun* became a favourite of the northern communities because of the regularity of her weekly calls and speed, sometimes arriving at Prince Rupert from Vancouver in under 48 hours. In July 1906 she barely escaped disaster running over Lima Reef in the uncharted section of Prince Rupert harbour, despite the presence of a government surveyor on her bridge. The *Camosun*'s double bottom kept her afloat, and she was returned to service in a month with full cabin bookings, her deck crowded with cannery workers. Carrying heavy general freight northbound, she brought canned salmon south on most trips. After Stewart was founded in 1907, the *Camosun* carried heavy equipment and men to the new mines of J.W. Stewart and the Portland Canal Development Company.

In May 1907 the *Camosun* was the first steamer on the Pacific coast to install Marconi wireless telegraph. Later, at Swanson Bay, she loaded the first pulp shipment from the Whalen Company's new mill, destined for Kobe, Japan. In January 1908 a petition by Prince Rupert residents secured the mail contract for the Union company because of the *Camosun*'s reliable schedules. Until five years after World War I the *Camosun* was regarded as the company's flagship, and her best-known navigator, Capt. Alfred E. Dickson, was recognized as "commodore" of the fleet.

A tragedy struck the company and Vancouver in the afternoon of 12 July 1906, now marked by the obelisk near Brockton Point in Stanley Park. The 60.0′ tug *Chehalis*, chartered by Robert Bryce and a party of seven and carrying a crew of eight, was sliced into and sunk by the *Princess Victoria*, which attempted to pass too closely on the south side of Burrard Inlet channel. Drowned were Mrs. Bryce, wife of the charterer; Dr. W.A.B. Hutton of the Rock Bay Hospital; the young son of J.O. Benwell; purser P.J. Chick; and four crewmen. There were miraculous rescues, but Capt. James House was left badly crippled. A marine commission placed responsibility on the *Princess Victoria,* and subsequent new harbour regulations prohibited ships from passing inside Burnaby Light.

With the northern coast now being adequately served, the Union reinforced the logging route where increased passenger demands far exceeded the combined accommodations of the *Cassiar* and the *Comox.* There were 16 settlements, with a small wharf or landing float and a combined store and post office, between Campbell River and the tip of Vancouver Island. Hunting and fishing parties also wanted transport upcoast, and early tourists sought adventure along the little-known routes of the Union line, which threaded the most entrancing but desolate waterways remaining to be explored on the North American continent.

In 1907 the company contracted with the Ailsa Shipbuilding Company of Troon, Ayrshire, for a new ship, the *Cariboo,* to serve the logging route or as a relief vessel for the northern run. She was 35.0′ shorter than the *Camosun* and about two-thirds her tonnage. Her bridge was set forward to give the navigator a clear view over the bow when coming alongside small camp floats and landings. The *Cariboo* reached Vancouver on 21 July 1908, after a good passage round The Horn under Capt. Charles Polkinghorne, but she was renamed the *Cowichan* when the chosen name was found to duplicate that of a Great Lakes vessel. Her accommodations, finished in white oak and mahogany, were far superior in quality and in the provision of much more cabin and saloon space than those of previous logging ships. "The Cow"—as the settlers nicknamed her—made twice-weekly sailings to Rock Bay, serving the main ports on Johnstone Strait as far as Alert Bay.

Pioneer A.M. (Fred) Wastell, Justice of the Peace at Telegraph Cove, remembered the *Cowichan:*

> To us she was a grand ship, and everyone wanted to go to town in her comfort. There were a score of points along Johnstone Strait and the off-channels between Vancouver and Beaver Cove where settlements could be found, or at which an old pioneer had built a landing float, and a store combining a post office. Each of these characters was a story in himself. His "kingdom," as that is what he made it, was ruled and governed by him—the only "fount" on activities, financial standing, or marital relations of all in his territory.

News came in August 1907 of the Grand Trunk Pacific's decision to make Prince Rupert their major northern terminal, and of their grandiose plan for Pacific liners to make connection there on a shorter global route. Gordon Legg extended the Carrall Street dock before the spring of 1908. He had planned to build two ships exceeding 200.0′, but cut back the length after the GTP in 1909 laid down two magnificent 300.0′ coast liners at the Tyneside yard at Wallsend.

The GTP also bought a ship and renamed her the *Prince Albert*—the first of the "Prince" fleet—to connect between Prince Rupert and the Queen Charlotte Islands, for which a federal subsidy had been granted. Their new liners *Prince Rupert* and *Prince George* reached the Pacific coast in June and July of 1910, respectively, and cornered the main share of the Prince Rupert terminal business, but called at only five major ports. It was almost four years later, on 8 April 1914, that the GTP rails (later Canadian National Railways) reached the Pacific coast.

While the continental GTP tracks (despite incredible terrain problems) were still pushing east to link with the tracks from Edmonton, the *Camosun* carried an enormous amount of supplies for the work crews, including "beef on the hoof"—wild range cattle stalled or tethered on the main deck. On several occasions cattle broke loose, chasing deckhands aloft until the stock was secured.

The smallest of the Union's new ships, the *Cheslakee,* was built by the Dublin Dockyard and arrived in Vancouver on 26 September 1910, looking like a tug, since her upper structure had not yet been built. Gordon Legg placed the contract for her upper-deck cabins and final alterations with the Wallace shipyard in North Vancouver. When put into service alongside the *Cowichan* and *Cassiar* on the logging route, the *Cheslakee* appeared to be a very stable vessel, although she tended to roll more heavily in foul weather than others in the fleet.

The year 1911 recorded the high-water mark of the company's achievement and expansion under Gordon Legg's regime. The Union had come a long way since its struggle to avoid bankruptcy, before the Klondike Gold Rush days and the coming of the *Cassiar* and the *Camosun.* The spring schedule of March 1911 reflected its growth. Eight red-and-black-funnelled ships (six passenger ships and the cargo vessels *Capilano* and *Coquitlam*) were listed as serving 118 ports of call, comprising 98 settlements and logging camps, and 20 unnamed canneries on the Nass and Skeena rivers, and at Rivers Inlet and Smith's Inlet.

There was a fast northern route served by the *Camosun,* leaving Wednesday nights on a 48-hour run between Vancouver and Prince Rupert and on to Stewart, described as "the hub of the newest and richest mineral district of British Columbia." Each week a cargo ship (alternately the *Capilano* and the *Coquitlam*) sailed from the Union pier, stopping with freight at any of 40 main ports en route to Prince Rupert and Stewart, and bringing cargoes south. There were six weekly logging-camp sailings, with the *Cassiar* using the Okis Hollow Channel to Minstrel Island and Kingcome Inlet, and the *Cheslakee* going via Lewis Channel to Port Neville or Welbore Channel.

In addition, the *Cowichan* made two trips weekly to Union Bay, Comox, and Campbell River, and to Nanaimo on Saturday nights. The *Cheslakee* served Lasqueti Island and Lund every Monday. The little *Comox* made three local trips each week, stopping at Roberts Creek, Wilson Creek, Flat Island, and Pender Harbour. She also served the Jervis Inlet camps twice a week, and Refuge Cove and Cortez Island on the third sailing. There were seven sailings a week to Powell River, and six to nearby Lund, also two or more weekly calls at 50 other stops. The routes covered over 5,000 miles a week, or 250,000 miles a year.

This 1911 schedule justifies the Union's reputation as "the upcoast streetcar line." It listed 18 ports where there were hotel accommodations: Prince Rupert, Stewart, Van Anda, Powell River, Campbell River, Rock Bay, Port Harvey, Union Bay, Courtenay, Beaver Creek, Nanaimo, Comox, Lund, Heriot Bay, Shoal Bay, Granite Bay, Minstrel Island, Pender Harbour.

The last ship to be laid down by Gordon Legg was the *Chelohsin,* at the Dublin Dockyard at the end of 1910, but while she was being built, the Union Steamship Company came under English ownership in mid-1911. News of the company's remarkable success had reached James Hughes Welsford, dynamic president of the Liverpool cargo line of J.H. Welsford & Co. Ltd., who promptly came to Vancouver and purchased controlling interest.

The price for the shares was in excess of $400,000, with an understanding that the Welsford company would undertake delivery of and pay for the 175.0′ vessel *Chelohsin.*

In September 1911 Welsford rounded off his new British Columbia interests by acquiring the Boscowitz Steamship Company of Victoria, with its two passenger and cargo vessels, *Vadso* and *Venture,* for $160,000. The latter vessel of 180.0′ was a fine cannery-type ship, built the preceding year in the Clyde shipyard of Napier & Miller. Its purchase gave the Union line control of the northern cannery business, and brought the amalgamated fleet to a total of 11 coastal steamers.

Welsford, a shrewd shipping man, already had American interests with a branch office at Galveston, Texas, and cargo liners of his Gulf Transport line operating in the Galveston-Liverpool cotton trade. He was looking ahead to the opening of the Panama Canal, and the prospect of using the Union coastal fleet as feeders for his Pacific cargoes. In August 1911 he sent Ernest H. Beazley, his highly qualified cargo superintendent at Liverpool, to Vancouver to become managing director of the Union Steamship Company. Beazley, who took over from Gordon Legg before the latter's retirement, was the son of J.H. Beazley, a leading Merseyside shipowner. He proved to be a first-class choice.

After the transfer of ownership, Welsford was elected Union president. Francis Carter-Cotton, MLA, a founding director, returned to the company as board chairman, and also became the first chancellor of the University of British Columbia the next year. Two leading officials who came over from the Boscowitz line, along with several captains and engineers, were John Barnsley and George McGregor. Barnsley, who had been Boscowitz's secretary-manager, was appointed northern (Prince Rupert) agent; six years later he was transferred south as assistant manager. McGregor, a major Boscowitz shareholder and owner of Victoria Tugboat Company, was the Union's Victoria agent for the next quarter-century, assisted latterly by Walter S. Miles.

On 29 December Ernest Beazley welcomed the arrival of the *Chelohsin,* and her four decks and splendid accommodations were greatly admired. She sailed north on 24 February 1912, under Captain Cowper with George Foster as chief engineer, to the Skeena River, Prince Rupert, and Goose Bay (later Anyox). It was the consensus of the Union's navigators that the *Chelohsin* was an excellent sea-boat, and that her facilities were surpassed by few other ships in the B.C. coast trade during this era. She became a favourite of travellers, including northern mining men.

Ernest Beazley undertook an extensive renovation of the Union dock and offices. The wharf was widened, a larger freight shed was built, and rail trackage was extended for unloading freight cars at dockside. A new engineering workshop adjoining the superintendent engineer's wharf office was built to improve carpentry and general repair work. The new manager was soon recognized as a leader in coast shipping circles and the Vancouver Board of Trade, and he and his wife, Elsie, became leaders in the city's community and social activities.

The *Cheslakee* sank alongside the Van Anda wharf in the early morning of 7 January 1913, with the loss of six passengers and a crew member. She had left Van Anda earlier for Powell River with 89 passengers. While crossing Malaspina Strait she was caught by a sudden squall and took on a dangerous list after shipping two heavy seas. Chief Officer Robert Wilson turned against the storm and headed back to Van Anda. Capt. John Cockle ordered all passengers to be roused, and when they reached Van Anda Cockle got a starboard line to the dock and ran out a gangway in blackness, the rising water having extinguished the lights. Despite his heroic efforts to get everyone ashore, the line snapped and within four minutes the vessel heeled. It is the only recorded loss of life on a scheduled Union passenger ship.

A court of enquiry censured the former Union head Gordon Legg for making structural additions on the *Cheslakee* without a new survey, although it appeared that the flooding resulted from failure to close the freight side-doors. The court also said that "the seamanship shown by the master, and pilot Robert Wilson, was commendable in avoiding a greater catastrophe."

The *Cheslakee* was salvaged and towed to Vancouver, then rebuilt, the hull being lengthened to give increased stability. To overcome nautical superstition, her name was changed to *Cheakamus* on returning to service five months later. She served for a further 25 years.

The *Cowichan* and the *Chelohsin* were now converted to oil-burning ships. As schedules permitted, conversions were made to the rest of the Union's expanded fleet except the *Cassiar,* which remained a coal-burner to her end. As well as improving operations and making for much cleaner ships, the conversions saved valuable coaling time at Union Bay and dispensed with the need to keep bunkering piles or coal bins at the end of the Union wharf.

With the addition of the Boscowitz ships, the Union's northern routes were now revised and strengthened. Beazley commissioned the colourful writer Aitken Tweedale to produce two folders to entice sportsmen and tourists to the B.C. coast—*Fin, Feather and Fur* and *North by West in the Sunlight.* The second title became an early company slogan. The new manager's plans for the fleet were progressing. He was well served by Capt. Alexander (Sandy) Walker, a dour Scot who came from one of Andrew Weir's big sailing ships. Sandy joined the company in 1907 as wharfinger at the Union terminal, and as marine superintendent for 30 years he earned an envied reputation.

Coast trade steadily expanded until 1914 with the development of Granby's huge copper mine and smelter at Anyox, a mining surge near Stewart, and new pulp mills at Ocean Falls and Powell River. But the outbreak of World War I depressed local trade and stifled industrial growth for a time as many Pacific ships were withdrawn to carry war supplies to Britain.

Two Union ships were lost during the war but not from enemy action. The freighter *Vadso* ran aground off the Nass River in a snowstorm on 3 February 1914 and was destroyed by fire when the oil cargo ignited. Capt. Larry Thompson and his crew abandoned ship and reached Arrandale Cannery without mishap. The freighter *Capilano,* one of the three pioneer Union ships, struck a rock off Texada Island on 30 September 1915 and sank early the next morning off Savary Island. Capt. Sam Nelson and his crew rowed ashore at Indian Point.

In a measure of wartime co-operation, and to ensure the production of airplane spruce from the Queen Charlotte Islands, the Union assumed operation of the GTP *Prince Albert* on a fortnightly route from Vancouver to the Charlottes via Prince Rupert. The Union's *Chelohsin* also took over one of the railway's two weekly sailings to Prince Rupert and maintained this rail connection throughout the war.

Several Union captains served in the British Admiralty's transport section, and Capt. John Cockle died overseas. More than 65 of the Union's marine and office personnel volunteered their services, including five mates and nine engineers who went to the Royal Navy. The freight agent, O. Fyson, was among those who did not return, and Capt. Francis Bannerman lost an arm. The Union's Capt. B.L. (Barney) Johnson commanded one of Canada's two submarines, and earned the D.S.O. for an exploit in the North Sea.

Within a month of America's entry into the war, James Hughes Welsford died in London after a brief illness at the age of 53. The Welsford company had lost three of its freighters to submarines, and two others were interned at Hamburg. Welsford's new chairman was Major George B. Haddock, MP. George S. Page and Arnold Rushton were appointed co-directors of the Welsford line in Liverpool, where Beazley went for consultations. Francis Carter-Cotton, who had become head of the Vancouver Harbour Commission, withdrew as chairman of the Union board and was succeeded by Grange V. Holt, manager of the Canadian Bank of Commerce.

Before Welsford died, the directors had discussed entry into the day-steamer trade. Beazley had suggested building a local steamer in 1912, when the new All-Red Line of Captain Polkinghorne and Sam Mortimer had only one ship, the *Selma,* running three trips weekly between Vancouver and Powell River. Welsford demurred at the time, but in January 1914 bought the 156.0' steamer *Melmore,* a Great Western Railway vessel that had been brought to the Pacific coast by Polkinghorne in 1913 and was laid up in North Vancouver. The Union used her for Empire Day excursions on 24 May 1914. She had a licence for 475 day passengers and operated day excursions to Pender Harbour, Seaside Park, and the Gulf Islands. Through June and July she ran Moonlight Cruises on Howe Sound and evening trips to Indian River with a string band. She was laid up, as a result of the war, in late 1914 and sold in 1916 to Peruvians.

The Union's plan to enter the resort trade was still alive when the authorized capital of the company was raised to $2,000,000 with the issue of additional preference and ordinary shares. A new charter was obtained in 1916 to permit investment in land. For three years, Ernest Beazley had arranged for Capt. John Cates to load and operate his Terminal Steam Navigation ships from the Union dock for Bowen Island and Howe Sound. This provided extra revenue, as well as a convenient "window" on the rapidly growing excursion business.

In October 1917 the Union Steamship Company paid $117,500 for the All-Red Line, whose two ships had derived much increased traffic from a dozen resorts and sizable communities between Vancouver and the growing pulp-and-paper town of Powell River. The two ships served the logging operations of Brooks, Scanlon & O'Brien at Stillwater, and smaller Jervis Inlet camps via Pender Harbour. Polkinghorne had added the *Santa Maria* after the *Selma,* and the look-alike former steam yachts, both built at Elder & Company's Glasgow yard, crisscrossed daily on the gulf coast, usually passing off Sechelt.

The purchase of the All-Red Line included seven acres of land at Selma Park, where a wharf landing had been built, a mile south of Sechelt on the other side of the Indian Reserve. the line had bought this small property partly as an alternative landing to Sechelt after a dispute over the cost of wharfage with Herbert Whitaker, whose estate extended over the waterfront. He had owned, in turn, three small vessels that operated to Sechelt from 1903 to 1914. The Selma land was the first real estate owned by the Union and it committed the company to future interest in summer excursions. The two ships added to the fleet were given Indian names beginning, as was customary, with the letter "C"—the *Selma* becoming the *Chasina* and the *Santa Maria* renamed the *Chilco.*

Among the well-known mariners who came to the company with these vessels were Howard E. Lawrey and Henry Roach (later captains) and purser George Read. It is clear that Beazley, in securing the key gulf coast route, aimed at keeping this promising area from becoming a base for competitors to enter the general coastal trade. In February 1918 he brought the former ferry *Washington* from Seattle, but quickly found her unsuitable for local service along the gulf coast. The ship was dismantled and the hull sold back to Seattle owners the following year, but the engines were retained.

A general boom in Pacific coast trade followed America's entry into the war, especially in shipbuilding to replace the heavy losses from submarine sinkings in the Atlantic. The boom brought a comparable increase in B.C.'s coastal business, and plans were drawn for new Union ships, including a freighter, to meet post-war needs.

Under Ernest Beazley's direction the Union company emerged from the war years a closely knit and highly respected organization in the Vancouver community. Its reliability through the years, and the nature of its friendly service in linking the early settlements with the outside world, made it a solid favourite with the coast people.

1889~1918

The Union Fleet in Photographs

CAMOSUN I
CAPILANO I
CASSIAR I
CHASINA
CHESLAKEE & CHEAKAMUS
CHEHALIS
CHELOHSIN
CHILCO & LADY PAM
COMOX I
COQUITLAM I
COUTLI
COWICHAN
CUTCH
LEONORA
MELMORE
ROTHESAY
SENATOR
SKIDEGATE
VADSO
VENTURE
WASHINGTON

1 *John Darling of Glasgow, Scotland, and New Zealand. Founder of the Union Steamship Co. of British Columbia Ltd. Director and retired general superintendent of the Union Steamship Co. of New Zealand.*

2 *Col. Alfred St. George Hamersley, first chairman of the Union Steamship Company and city solicitor.*

3 *Hon. Francis Lovet Carter-Cotton, chairman, 1911 to 1917. MLA. Publisher of Vancouver's* Daily News & Advertiser. *First chancellor of University of British Columbia.*

1   2   3

4 *The S.S.* Senator, *circa 1889–90, beside float at the city wharf, foot of Carrall Street, about to depart for Moodyville Sawmill across Burrard Inlet. Named in honour of Senator Hugh Nelson.*

4

5 *The tug Leonora. Engaged in early Vancouver harbour towing and ferry service before the* Senator *was built.*

6 *The tug Skidegate, alongside the original Union wharf ticket office and waiting room in 1889. Used for upcoast towing and as a relief ferry, especially after her new passenger saloon was built in 1891.*

7 *Union Steamship Company's wharf and office, 1 July 1890. Passengers have boarded a scow which will be towed by the Skidegate to a small wharf at Hallelujah Point for the Dominion Day games at Brockton Point grounds, Stanley Park. Large vessel in background is believed to be the 326.0' City of Puebla which ran between Victoria and San Francisco.*

5

6

7

8 *The steamer* Cutch *in Vancouver harbour after arrival from India, 1890.*

9 *1892 advertisement for the S.S.* Cutch.

10 *The* Cutch *coming into Skagway after having been rebuilt for Alaska service in 1898. Note single funnel.*

8

9

UNION STEAMSHIP CO., B. C. LT'D.

Head Office and Wharf, Vancouver, B. C.

VANCOUVER AND NANAIMO DAILY.

SS. Cutch Leaves C. P. R. Wharf at 1.00 p. m., returning from Nanaimo at 7 a. m. Cargo received at Union SS. Co's. wharf, Vancouver, until noon.

TOURISTS' TICKETS

Are issued for round trip from Vancouver and return via Nanaimo, Esquimalt & Nanaimo Railway to Victoria, and return by E. & N. Ry. or by C. P. N. Co's. steamers from Victoria to Vancouver. Fare, Round Trip, $6.00.

VANCOUVER and PORTLAND, ORE.
Carrying Freight and Passengers.

SS. Taichiow (1300 tons). This steamer makes fortnightly trips between Vancouver and Portland, via Victoria Sound ports and Astoria.

☞Small steamers and scows always available for excursion, towing and freighting business. Ample storage and accommodation on Co's wharf. Contracts taken. All particulars on application to office.

Union SS. Co., B. C., Vancouver.

William Webster,   Manager.

TELEPHONE 94.   P. O. BOX 217.

10

11

12 *The* Cutch *in 1892 carrying a party of Vancouver's notable citizens on a day's outing. (centre back l-r) Capt. P.H. Johnson, W.J. Meakin.(middle l-r) O.G. Evan Thomas, Mr. McKee, Edward Mahon, John Mahon, C.T. Dunbar, H.A. Jones, Sir John Reid, Isaac Oppenheimer, G.G. Mackay, George Turner, Otto Semisch, J.T. Williams, Mr. Oppenheimer, W. Sully, G.V. Holt, Lindsay Phillips. (front l-r) Colonel Barwis, G.D. Mackay, H.T. Ceperley, S.O. Richards, Mr. Fry, T.H. Calland, Thomas Dunn, J.C. Keith. (seated on hatch) H. Abbott (general superintendent of the CPR).*

13 *The company's first logging-camp vessel, the* Comox, *showing upper-deck cabins.*

14 *The* Comox *in 1892, lying off Bowen Island.*

15 *The* Comox *on a local weekend excursion, July 1898.*

16 *The Union's first freighter, the* Capilano, *towing the steamer* Lightning *in St. Michael's Harbour, Alaska. She carried both livestock and passengers during the gold rush.*

13

14

15

16

17 *Poster advertisement of the S.S. Capilano's departure August 1897 for Alaska.*

18 *Capt. Ernest A. Powys of the* Capilano, *the first British vessel to sail to the Klondike in 1897.*

19 *Capt. John Park at age 92, oldest living master mariner of the Union company. He is now in his 100th year.*

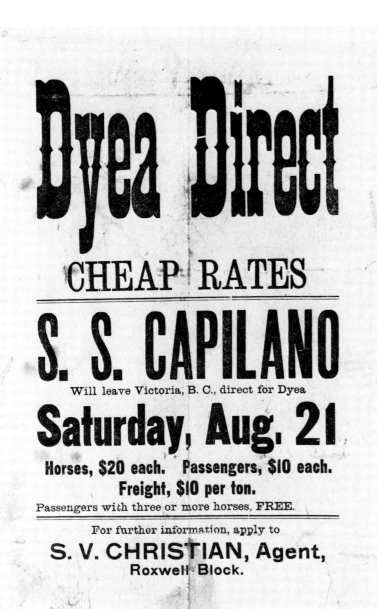

17

18

19

20 *The* Coquitlam *berthing, circa 1910. She was the first Vancouver vessel to regularly serve the Rivers Inlet and Skeena River canneries.*

21 *The stern-wheeler* Rothesay, *built in 1898 as a passenger ferry for the Stikine River during the gold rush. She was found unsuitable for outside waters, and was chartered by the Union company for harbour and North Arm excursions.*

22 *The S.S.* Coquitlam, *one of the earliest vessels of the Union Steamship Company, in Vancouver harbour, 1892.*

20

21

22

23 *Strip of commuter's tickets for the Union's North Vancouver ferry service, around 1898.*

24 *The* Cassiar *as the* J.R. McDonald *in 1890.*

25 *The* Cassiar *about 1903 at the wharf of a Johnstone Strait logging stop. She was known as The Loggers' Palace, and literally charted the early logging route by bumping into a few rocks.*

23

24

25

26 *The S.S.* Camosun *at Margaret Bay in 1927.*

27 *The S.S.* Camosun *northbound to the Nass River and Stewart.*

28 *The* Camosun *leaving the old Campbell River wharf in 1907. Quadra Island's first ferry is alongside the wharf.*

29 *The* Camosun *was the first coast vessel to land at Prince Rupert, 27 April 1906. Canvas-covered shack in right foreground is the city's first post office.*

26

27

28

29

30 *The only existing photograph of the*
   ill-fated Chehalis, *taking out a special*
   charter party in Vancouver's harbour.

31 *The Union's last towboat,* Coutli, *entering Burrard Inlet with a log boom, about 1907.*

32 *The* Cheslakee, *rebuilt and renamed the* Cheakamus.

33 *The* Cheslakee *makes a float landing in Lewis Channel.*

34 *The* Cheslakee *heeled alongside Van Anda wharf, 7 January 1913.*

32

33

34

35 *The* Vadso *at the Boscowitz line wharf in Victoria Harbour before being taken over by the Union Steamship Company in 1911.*

36 *The* Cowichan *as the* Cariboo *(her name was later changed because of a duplication) running her speed trials off Scotland's Ayrshire coast.*

37 *The* Cowichan *in 1908 arriving on the B.C. coast.*

36

35

37

38 The Venture *operating under Boscowitz colours about 1911.*

39 The Venture *at a float landing in 1916.*

40 The Venture *docked at the Union wharf after unloading canned salmon.*

41 *(left) Bert Robson, one of the Union's best-known pursers. (right) Capt. John Park, the* Venture's *master; he later commanded Atlantic freighters.*

38

39

40

41

42 *The* Chelohsin *unloading at the main Rock Bay logging call with a boom alongside.*

44 *The* Melmore *arrived on the B.C. coast from Britain in 1913 and was converted for excursion service the next summer, running day and moonlight excursions to the accompaniment of a string band. Her last run was Labour Day, 1914.*

45 *The All-Red Line's* Selma.

46 *The* Selma *under Union colours and renamed* Chasina *leaving Vancouver harbour entrance.*

44

45

46

47 *The Union Steamship Company's 1917 calendar showing the fleet and the famous slogan "North by West in the Sunlight."*

44

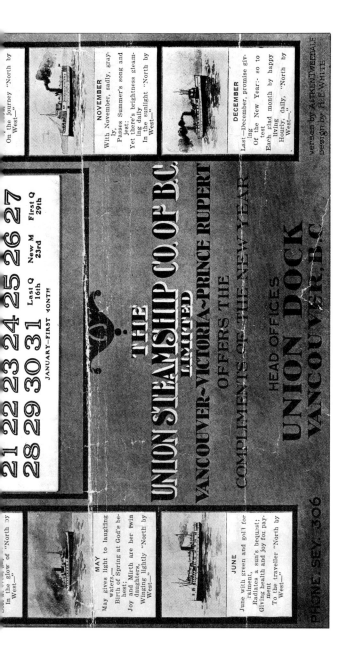

On the journey "North by West—"

NOVEMBER
With November, sadly, gray-
ly,
Passes Summer's song and
jest.
Yet there's brightness gleam-
ing daily
In the sunlight "North by
West—"

DECEMBER
Last—December, promise giv-
ing
Of the New Year: so to
test
Each glad month by happy
living
Hourly, daily, "North by
West—"

verses by AITKEN TWEEDALE
design by H. E. WHITE

21 22 23 24 25 26 27
28 29 30 31
Last Q   New M   First Q
16th   23rd   29th
JANUARY—FIRST MONTH

THE
UNION STEAMSHIP CO. OF B.C.
LIMITED
VANCOUVER~VICTORIA~PRINCE RUPERT
OFFERS THE
COMPLIMENTS OF THE NEW YEAR

HEAD OFFICES
UNION DOCK
VANCOUVER, B.C.

PHONE: SEY. 306

In the glow of "North by
West—"

MAY
May gives light to laughing
waters,—
Birth of Spring at God's be-
hest;
Joy and Mirth are her twin
daughters,
Winging lightly "North by
West—"

JUNE
June with green and golf for
raiment,
Radiates a sun's bequest;
Giving health and joy for pay-
ment
To the traveller "North by
West—"

48 *The* Chilco *renamed* Lady Pam *after her accommodation was rebuilt in 1935.*

49 *The* Chilco *entering Vancouver harbour, about 1918.*

50 *The* Washington. *She was given a brief trial as an excursion vessel in 1918 but was found unsuitable.*

48

49

50

1919-1939

" The Upcoast Streetcar Line "

Industrial expansion on the Pacific northwest coast following World War I emphasized the Union fleet's need for more freight tonnage to move lumber and heavier cargoes north and to bring more canned salmon south, as well as to transport ore concentrates in bulk from the Belmont Surf Inlet mine on the west side of Princess Royal Island, 65 miles north of Milbanke Sound. There was also increasing activity at the Anyox mine and at the Swanson Bay, Ocean Falls, and Powell River pulp plants. To capitalize on these opportunities, Ernest Beazley bought the 170.0' steel freighter *British Columbia* from the Coastwise Tugboat & Barge Company on 10 January 1919, and renamed her the *Chilliwack.*

Later in 1919, Beazley ordered construction of two vessels in Vancouver shipyards to designs by Henry Darling. A day steamer, the *Capilano II,* 146.0' overall, was laid down at B.C. Marine Ways. Her hull was of the finest Douglas fir and her main engine and auxiliary machinery came from the discarded *Washington.* She had a comfortable saloon and a fully open upper deck to warrant a licence for 350 summer excursionists and was designed to serve the local gulf coast and to promote the Union's Selma Park resort. She was launched on 20 December 1919.

The second new vessel, the steel freighter *Chilkoot,* 180.0' overall, was built at the Wallace shipyard in North Vancouver. Beazley's cargo expertise made this fast freighter with stowage for 20,000 cases of canned salmon the envy of the coast. She had convenient working hatches and a 20-ton lift capacity. At economical speed her tanks provided fuel for 3,000 miles, the distance of two northern round trips. She was launched on 26 February 1920.

No finer action is recorded in the marine annals of the B.C. coast than the superb seamanship of Capt. Charles B. Smith and the heroism of his engineers working in a flooded engine-room, when they saved the *Chilliwack* from disaster on the morning of 26 December 1919. On Christmas Day the *Chilliwack* had finished loading ore concentrates at Surf Inlet, consigned to the Tacoma smelter, but because she sailed late that night the wet ore had frozen solid after being stowed in sub-zero weather. By early morning the concentrates thawed and became a liquid menace when the vessel was struck by heavy seas off Day Point. She took a heavy list and almost heeled before reaching Milbanke Sound. The *Chilliwack* appeared doomed, but Captain Smith remembered a tiny sand cove nearby, scarcely bigger than the ship, and succeeded in beaching her there. For three days the crew drained the ore and restowed it, using logs from the beach as dividers, while Chief Engineer Fred Smith took the engines down and reoiled them. The *Chilliwack* was refloated on a high tide and discharged in Tacoma without having been seriously damaged. Captain Smith's skill and courage won recognition from Lloyd's of London.

The pioneer *Comox* was retired in 1919 and sold for scrap, but the hull was in such good condition that it was then sold and converted to a motor vessel for Mexican waters. A new *Capilano—Capilano II*—made her trial trip on 1 May 1920, to Selma Park with 300 guests, thus fulfilling Beazley's dream.

Union sailings had been interrupted by labour troubles for a week in 1917, and again briefly in June 1919. In mid-May 1920 a seamen's strike in another coastal line spread to the Union fleet. The company was forced to tie up all vessels as they reached port a few days before the 24 May weekend, leaving the Union dock silent over the holiday. Negotiations were progressing and Beazley expected an early settlement when he attended a special meeting in the city on Sunday evening, 23 May. An agreement was reached, but before it could be implemented Ernest Beazley was killed in a plane accident on 24 May at Minoru Park in Richmond. He had not planned to fly that day but, being president of the local flying club, was encouraged to take a ride with a visiting barnstorming pilot who crashed. Ernest Beazley was only 40 years of age, and was beloved and trusted by his employees and respected throughout the city and upcoast communities.

The funeral was held at Vancouver's Christ Church Cathedral and attended by leaders of the city and province, and by his office staff and the entire personnel of the Union fleet. Crowds lined Georgia Street as the cortege passed, with 16 uniformed Union captains marching alongside. The waterfront lay silent. Robert Kenmuir wrote in the Vancouver *Province:* "The flags of the vessels in the harbour may well be half-masted, for one who loved ships and the men who man them has gone out with the tide."

His passing deeply affected me. I had been sent from Liverpool in late April 1920 to gain experience under Mr. Beazley, and I was his house guest on 23 May. After supper, he was called to a strike meeting but before leaving told me his plans for further development of the coast trade with modern ships, and his hopes for the recent new vessels, the Selma resort, and the expanding summer prospects. He stressed with enthusiasm the all-round "people" service the company was providing on the coastal routes. Then he read from his notebook a list of Indian names that he had chosen for future Union ships. I like to feel that my inclusion of such names and their colourful meanings at the back of this book is a sort of personal memorial to Ernest Beazley.

The Union board appointed Beazley's assistant, John Barnsley, acting manager. In early August representatives of the J.H. Welsford Company arrived to look into the Union's affairs. They were my father, Arnold Rushton (later Sir Arnold and Lord Mayor of Liverpool), and Richard A.H. Welsford, son of the late principal owner. They made a round trip of the lower coast, looked over the company's business in Victoria, inspected the latest developments at the Selma Park resort, and travelled with Barnsley and Capt. John A. Cates to Bowen Island to inspect the latter's large estate and resort properties. John Barnsley was appointed general manager.

Selma Park had been transformed into an attractive small resort, with 20 cottages and additional tent sites. A fine dance pavilion, on a magnificent site overlooking the gulf, was opened in 1920, with a tearoom and store. Boats were available for fishing, and land was cleared for a picnic ground. On 16 June the new *Capilano* began day trips on a tri-weekly basis to Selma Park via Gower Point, Wilson Creek, and Roberts Creek. The schedule was extended at weekends to Halfmoon Bay (Redroofs) and Buccaneer Bay.

The new *Chilkoot* began her cargo service in June to the northern canneries and Prince Rupert, calling at Alert Bay, Namu, and way ports. Under command of Capt. James Findlay, she carried a crew of 20 including 6 deck officers and engineers. The pilot, as the line's chief officers were called, was "Chips" Williams. Her chief engineer was John Hogan, known for his Merseyside wit. It was said, with some truth, that the Union's engineers hailed from Glasgow or Liverpool, and its skippers from the Atlantic Provinces and Newfoundland or the Scottish west coast and Shetland Islands.

The *Chilkoot* was welcomed at Prince Rupert, where her coal was discharged. Described in guides as "the metropolis of the north," Prince Rupert was still in its boardwalk days, and recovering slowly from a wartime halt in building. The vessel earned her keep at this stage of the salmon-canning season by landing large loads of tinplate and supplies at a dozen wharves in the Skeena and off the entrance to the Nass River. Close to all landings were similar cannery buildings, low and white, where Indians and Orientals of both sexes worked between May and September.

On her maiden voyage, the *Chilkoot* called at Claxton, Port Essington, Cunninghams, and Haysport in the Skeena slough, and at Wales Island, Mill Bay, and Kumeon canneries at the Nass entrance. On the southbound voyage through Douglas Channel mail and a month's supplies were put off at the Indian village wharf at Kitimaat (as the charts spelled it). The addition of the *Chilkoot* to the freighter *Chilliwack's* scheduled run provided—for the first time—the basis for a weekly heavy cargo service of lumber, machinery, steel, and oil products to B.C.'s new plants, mills, and communities.

The Union Steamship Company became fully engaged in the resort and excursion business in December 1920 when it acquired the Bowen Island resort property of nearly 1,000 acres from Capt. John Cates, together with the business and steamers of his Terminal Steam Navigation Company, at a cost of about $250,000. John Cates, one of five seafaring brothers, had skippered small tugs on Howe Sound since 1897, and entered into the freight and passenger business to the head of Howe Sound two years later with the *Defiance*. In 1900 he bought the old Mannion ranch adjacent to Bowen's Snug Cove landing and developed a resort for summer camping and large picnics. He added acreage in the cove and around Deep Bay, where he built his Terminal Hotel and a dairy farm. With the new *Britannia*, he started the popular Bowen excursion trade in 1902 under the flag of the Terminal Company, operating to Britannia Mine and way calls to Squamish. In 1920, Squamish was the projected southern terminal of the Pacific Great Eastern Railway, then under construction to the northern interior of the province.

On the night of 13 November, several days before the sale was completed, one of Cates's two vessels, the *Ballena*, was destroyed by fire alongside the Union dock. His other ship, the *Bowena* (the former *City of Nanaimo*), was so badly damaged that it was May 1921 before she was ready to enter the Union's service under the name *Cheam*. Meanwhile, the *Capilano* had taken over the daily service on the East Howe Sound route to Squamish via Bowen Island, Britannia Beach, and Woodfibre, site of the Whalen Company's pulp plant.

An extensive building program got under way at the company's new Bowen estate, and work was pushed to get the improved facilities ready for the excursion season. A spacious pavilion, then the largest on the B.C. coast, capable of accommodating 800 couples on a circular dance floor with a central bandstand, was built in a charming woodland setting close to the steamer landing and opened on 24 May 1921. One hundred bungalows and smaller cottages replaced most of the old tent camps. The hotel was renovated and renamed Mt. Strahan Lodge for the mountain peak facing it directly across Howe Sound. Later the farm was upgraded with an imported herd of fine Ayrshire cattle. The *Cheam* and the *Capilano* were filled to capacity every summer weekend, and sometimes on other days, for two more seasons after 1921 before larger Union ships were built.

The Sannie Transportation Company began a ferry service in 1920 between Horseshoe Bay and Snug Cove on Bowen Island, with a single launch owned by J. Hilton Brown and named *Sannie* after an Australian racehorse that had brought him luck. Demand became so heavy that in May 1921 a scheduled service was put into operation with three "Sannies" for the summer season. Soon afterwards, the service was taken over by one of Brown's partners, T.D. (Tommy) White, and in 1925 the Sannie Company received a provincial charter for the ferry crossing. Until 1944, Tommy White operated independently but always in a friendly arrangement with the Union Steamship Company. In 1921 the PGE Railway started a local passenger service from its North Vancouver station along a west shore line to Horseshoe Bay, and this continued until a highway was extended to Whytecliff and the shores of Howe Sound in 1928. Thousands of visitors reached Bowen Island by this alternative route: PGE line and a Sannie ferry.

When the railway was completed to Quesnel in 1921, John Barnsley arranged to connect with the PGE at Squamish by a special steamer sailing, but the business proved unprofitable. The Union then contracted with the railway to make twice-weekly connections northbound and southbound by the regular Squamish steamer, with through-rail passengers and express. The PGE handled its own rail freight from the outset by barge between North Vancouver and the Squamish terminal.

After a recession in 1921, general coast trade picked up. The Union's northern passenger ships and freighters had a profitable cannery season in 1922, bringing south one of the largest salmon packs ever recorded on the B.C. coast.

The early 1920s saw a peak in the service provided to the upcoast pioneers by the Union's handy vessels. Jack Hetherington reflected it in his "Ship Shop" column in the North Vancouver *Times:* "Carrying passengers and groceries into virtually every nook and cranny on the B.C. coast, ships of the Union fleet provided a tangible link from southern 'civilization' to the far northern suburbs."

In summer 1922 the *Camosun,* under Capt. Alfred Dickson, made the scenic intermediate weekly trip to Rivers Inlet, Bella Coola, Kimsquit, and Ocean Falls, passing through the magnificent Dean Channel and stopping at 20 different settlements and canneries. After Alert Bay, one call was at Shushartie Bay cannery on the tip of Vancouver Island, where in dense fog the vessel once was piped to a safe landing by the cannery net boss, an old Scottish piper. Fishermen and trappers trudged miles to get mail and supplies at the wharf, one man in his haste stepping on a cougar dozing by the side of the rough trail.

On Rivers Inlet—an entrancing stretch of slate-blue water branching eastwards, with towering snow-capped peaks for a backdrop—the *Camosun* made calls from morning to late afternoon. She discharged supplies and mail at the main B.C. Packers' Wadhams cannery stop, and at Wallace Fisheries' Strathcona, Bell-Irving's Good Hope, and Canadian Fishing's Kildala canneries before exiting through the north entrance of Schooner Passage beyond J.H. Todd's Beaver cannery.

At all points, the Union crews and residents, many of the latter trooping aboard, shouted greetings, and passengers got a hearty welcome ashore. It was the moment of joyous contact for lonely souls with the outside world.

In command of the *Venture,* assigned to the main cannery route, Capt. Andrew Johnstone, on 16 September 1922, boldly rescued under perilous conditions all the passengers of the wrecked Seattle liner *Queen.* Southbound from Alaska, she had run aground early that morning in dense fog on Whitecliff Island off Prince Rupert. Captain Johnstone picked up the distress call at 5 A.M. while loading at the North Pacific Cannery on the Skeena River. He took his ship out in the fog and, using pinpoint navigation and whistle sounds for 12 miles, brought the *Venture* close astern to the stranded vessel. From the forward deck of his ship he hoisted a gangway over the stern of the *Queen,* where her passengers were clustered, and took off 238 relieved travellers, later landing them at Prince Rupert.

John Barnsley was appointed managing director of the Union company in October 1922, with Richard Welsford assuming the less active role of president before returning to England that fall. Welsford announced that the fleet would be augmented for the 1923 season by a new and larger steamer to operate on a fast time-table between Vancouver, Prince Rupert, and Anyox via intermediate ports of call. The contract for the new ship was let to Napier & Miller, who had built the *Venture* for the Boscowitz line at their Old Kilpatrick yard on the Clyde in 1910.

The new vessel, the *Cardena*—the first of two Spanish coast names to be adopted for the fleet—was planned as a prototype. She was 50.0' longer than the *Venture* and had much superior passenger accommodations including well-appointed drawing and smoking rooms, and outside staterooms, several with deluxe features. Her cargo space for 350 tons included a refrigeration chamber for 30 tons of boxed fish and capacity for 11,000 cases of canned salmon. The *Cardena* was launched on 22 March 1923. After exceeding 14 knots on her trial trip, she sailed for Vancouver under Capt. A.E. Dickson on 3 May, arriving on 11 June. The *Cardena* proved to be the finest sea-boat and the most popular vessel to fly the Union flag, and brought to 12 the number of the company's ships having a gross tonnage exceeding 10,500 tons.

The *Cardena* sailed under Captain Johnstone on her maiden voyage on 28 July to Prince Rupert and the Skeena and Nass rivers. The *Chelohsin* was placed in the principal logging-camp service along Johnstone Strait, while the *Cowichan* and the *Cheakamus* served Kingcome, Bute, and Knight inlets, as well as the inside waterways where smaller settlements were located. This enabled the *Cassiar* to be retired. Two older

vessels, the *Chasina* and the *Coquitlam,* were also sold at this time. The *Chasina* operated illicitly as a rum-runner for five years, and in 1931 after leaving Hong Kong disappeared in an unsolved sea mystery. The *Coquitlam* should have been broken up or sold away from this coast, because she came back as the *Bervin* to run for a decade in competition with the Union.

In May 1923 Richard Welsford announced that a large day steamer was being laid down for the Bowen Island and Howe Sound trade, with a greater carrying facility than that of any similar vessel north of San Francisco. William D. McLaren, head of the Coaster Construction Co. of Montrose, Scotland, arrived in Vancouver in the summer to settle final plans for the new steamer with Barnsley and Welsford. In October, the keel of the future famed *Lady Alexandra* was laid. She was 235.0' overall, with a dining room that seated 86 and also served as a dancing floor. She became the best-known excursion vessel to operate out of Vancouver, and was the first of four Union steamers to be built or converted at Montrose's Rossie Island yard under W.D. McLaren's supervision. He later became a founder of West Coast Shipbuilders Ltd. in Vancouver.

Both the northern and local ships of the company ran close to capacity through the 1923 season. John Barnsley was not in good health and needed experienced executive assistance, especially for the development of the Union Estates on Bowen Island and in promoting business for the new steamers in advance of their arrival. On 8 September Harold Brown, who had a broad transportation background, was appointed assistant general manager.

With increasing demands for passenger service on the gulf coast, and a critical need for another Howe Sound steamer, the company bought a 480-passenger ship, the *Lady Evelyn,* which had been built at Birkenhead in 1901 as the *Deerhound.*

She was brought to Vancouver in 1922 by the Howe Sound Navigation Co. and had carried large excursions to Seaside Park for two seasons. The *Lady Evelyn* was the first of the Union's "Lady" steamers. This prefix, used only for day steamers, distinguished them in the public mind from the fleet's trading vessels.

An illustrated booklet entitled *Our Coastal Trips* was published in 1922 to advertise the coming of the *Cardena* and the tourist trips available on six routes through little-known waterways. Some of the splendid new facilities at Bowen Park were also depicted. Harold Brown took the publicity and traffic division of the company under his wing in late 1923. He streamlined the public information office and set in motion an imaginative promotional program that created a boom in excursions and day trips.

The *Lady Alexandra* was launched on 21 February 1924, and left for the Pacific coast on 7 May under Capt. C.B. Smith. This splendid 1,400-licensed carrier for day trips on inside waters was welcomed to Vancouver harbour on 21 June. She made her first excursion four days later with 800 sightseers to greet H.M.S. *Hood*'s arrival on a special visit to the city. The *Lady Alexandra* became such a favourite on outings to the head of Howe Sound, and especially so to thousands of young people picnicking at Bowen Island, that she was enthroned as the city's Excursion Queen over the next two decades.

Actually the company had erred in its specifications for the *Lady Alexandra*. A lot more passenger space and trimmer lines could have been obtained had the company not insisted on an immense forehold and 'tween-deck space for packing salmon south after the excursion season. This was tried only once and the vessel proved unsuitable for exposed waters.

The extra passenger capacity and faster speed that were needlessly sacrificed could have dramatically improved her profit in the peak cruising months. A cargo space of 300 tons was far too much; 100 tons was more than enough for the *Lady Alexandra,* or for any of the day steamers.

John Barnsley died on 19 August 1924, within a year of Harold Brown's appointment as his assistant. In four years, Barnsley had achieved outstanding financial results with his shrewd operational judgements and long freighting experience in the northern trade. A newspaper described him as "an honest, aggressive business man with a kind heart toward all." Perhaps his most valuable contribution to the Union line was in planning the *Cardena,* already an established favourite throughout the north. Harold Brown succeeded him and presided over the company's greatest expansion during the next five years.

In the fall of 1924, President Richard Welsford contracted again with McLaren's Montrose yard for a northern ship, the *Catala,* and the conversion of two former minesweepers, *Swindon* and *Barnstaple,* to the future day steamers *Lady Cecilia* and *Lady Cynthia.* The twin vessels were constructed with large enclosed saloons, and side sponsons were attached to their hulls amidships to provide stability for the addition of an open upper deck, and for the carrying of 900 excursionists. The *Catala* had very similar passenger and cargo capacity to that of the *Cardena,* but was much different in appearance. She had two funnels and a wide upper promenade deck that circled the ship and was the delight of summer tourists. At a distance, her silhouette gave the impression of a miniature ocean liner. Her sea-going qualities were excellent, although she was a "stiffer ship" than the *Cardena.* The *Catala* was launched on 25 February, and on the same day the *Lady Cecilia* was christened alongside an adjoining pier.

The *Lady Cecilia* was completed well ahead of the northern ship, and arrived at Vancouver on 14 April. She was first assigned to daily service on the Squamish route. The *Catala* followed on 12 July 1925, and left the Union pier on 29 July for Prince Rupert and northern ports. She was ferried from Montrose by Capt. James Findlay, who then returned to Scotland to bring out the *Lady Cynthia,* which entered Vancouver harbour on 22 August to begin her service on Howe Sound. The *Lady Cecilia* ran daily trips along the gulf coast to Pender Harbour, remaining under the command of Capt. Neil Gray until 1937. Their size (they were licensed for 900) and speed enabled each of these sister ships to carry the larger companies' employees in less than two hours to enjoy their sports and facilities at the spacious Selma Park ground and later at nearby Sechelt.

A salt-water swimming pool was now a popular feature at Bowen Park, the summer cottages now exceeded 100, and new covered tables were in use on four picnic grounds. The tearoom had been enlarged and a general store of artistic design was planned. Most of Vancouver's largest firms held their employees' annual outing at Bowen Island. The Port of Vancouver was closed on one Wednesday in mid-July each year to all cargo movements because of the International Longshoremen's Union picnic at Bowen Park. All the picnic grounds were reserved for the more than 3,000 waterfront workers and their families who embarked on the Union's three day boats with prodigious supplies for a day of sports and fun.

A novelty of the summer was the Sea-and-Rail Day Trip on Sundays, run in conjunction with the PGE Railway to Alta Lake for a return fare of $2.50. It combined the Howe Sound cruise with a transfer to open rail cars at Squamish for a spectacular ride through the Cheakamus Canyon. The Union's cruise was promoted by a map folder entitled *The Magical Day Sea-Trip on Howe Sound.* A coloured pictorial folder, with a map showing all the resorts to Pender Harbour and as far as Savary Island, was entitled *Sunshine and Sea-Charm Along the Gulf Coast Riviera.* Harold Brown originated the name Sunshine Coast, long since adopted for this entrancing stretch of coast. *The Lure of the Coast Sea-Trails* was the title of another illustrated folder, with a coast map, that described the six-day northern cruises of the *Cardena* and the *Catala.*

Harold Brown's program for the Union Estates' Bowen Island development focussed on the renovation of Mt. Strahan Lodge, and improvement of the resort's recreational facilities. Loads of golden sand were brought from Scotland's east coast as ballast in the holds of the *Lady Alexandra* and the *Catala,* and spread over Bowen's main bathing beach, opposite the hotel in Deep Bay. A children's play area was added near the sandy beach, six hard tennis courts adjoining the lodge were brought up to championship standard, and saddle horses were made available at the farm stables for trail-riding.

From the mid-1920s, with the coming of the *Lady Cecilia* and the *Lady Cynthia,* Vancouver overflowed on summer weekends with holidayers bound for Bowen Island and the chain of resorts developing along the shores of West Howe Sound and the gulf coast.

The exodus from the city began on special Friday night steamers, which became known as The Daddy Boats. Thousands of weekenders left the Union pier summer-long for Gibsons, Granthams, and Hopkins, for Roberts Creek, Selma Park, and Sechelt, but with the majority headed for Bowen Island. From early June the day ships carried camp groups to the YMCA's Camp Elphinstone and to church camps at Gambier Island, Keats Island, and Hopkins Landing. The gulf steamer carried many Boy Scouts, Girl Guides, and Brownies to Roberts Creek and Wilson Creek.

The Union vessels were almost the only means of travel for camp cottagers along the Lower Mainland coast, which was still unconnected by main roads.

On the night of 27 December 1925, the *Cowichan,* returning slowly south with only 14 passengers, was almost sliced in two and sank within seven minutes after being rammed in fog off Roberts Creek by the *Lady Cynthia,* northbound with an extra load of Christmas visitors returning to Powell River. Capt. John Boden held the bow of his vessel pinned into the *Cowichan* until all 45 passengers and crew had clambered to safety over the rail of his foredeck. A.W. (Al) Newman, freight clerk on the *Cowichan,* and later a general agent of the company, recalled the accident thus:

> It all happened between 9:20 and 9:27 P.M. After helping the last of his crew overside, Capt. Robert Wilson stepped onto the *Lady Cynthia's* deck and shouted to Boden on the bridge, "Pull her out now, Cap, or she'll take us down with her!" It seemed only moments after the vessels parted that the *Cowichan* went down by the stern, and her bow shot up out of the water. After the crash the fog suddenly cleared.

The loss of the *Cowichan,* with plenty of service life ahead, upset the company's lower-coast schedules for a time. However, the *Chelohsin* and the *Venture,* with seasonal northern reliefs, were now mainly being used on the logging-port routes, covering an area up to Seymour Inlet.

In April 1926 the Union company bought 240 acres of land at Sechelt from the Whitaker estate. The deal included central waterfront property comprising the hotel, a tearoom, a large general store and warehouse, and considerable adjacent acreage partly cleared and available for cottages and resort development. Herbert Whitaker had purchased the land to operate a trading post, and in 1889 he built the original hotel. The property was separated from Selma Park by the Indian Reserve in the half-moon of Trail Bay (hence the name of nearby Halfmoon Bay). The Indian village was earlier sited on Porpoise Bay, but was moved to the seaward side of the peninsula when French priests established the mission there in 1900. Before the All-Red Line had begun service, Whitaker operated several small vessels between Vancouver and Sechelt in charge of Capt. Sam Mortimer.

Harold Brown reconditioned the Sechelt Hotel and laid out a large picnic ground with sufficient facilities to cater to the largest city organizations. It was intended to promote day excursions and offer an alternative venue to Bowen Park for the growing picnic trade. Sixteen new cottages were planned, with new tennis courts and good fishing and bathing conveniences. George Aman, the Union's general agent, remained at Sechelt for another two years, when he was succeeded by Robert S. Hackett.

A radical change in the Union company's corporate structure took effect in January 1926. After 37 years, the Union Steamship Company of British Columbia ceased to function as an operating company, and instead held the stock of two subsidiary companies: Union Steamships Limited, formed for ship operations; and Union Estates, formed to develop the land holdings and resorts at Bowen and Selma, and to operate the Sechelt properties.

The freighter *Chilliwack* was sold the same year. As her replacement to operate alongside the *Chilkoot,* the larger and faster *Ardgarvel* was purchased in Scotland and refitted on the Clyde before being "ferried out" to Vancouver by Captain Findlay. This powerful ship, renamed *Chilliwack II,* with a 1,100-ton cargo capacity, could handle the longest steel and pack up to 28,000 cases of canned salmon. She was put into cargo service to northern B.C. ports on 31 May 1927.

A significant change took place in coast lumbering towards the end of the 1920s as the era of hand-logging passed into history. While scores of small logging operations continued along the inside channels, the trend was to centralize production and log assembly through larger ports, where the major companies, for whom many smaller logging companies worked on contract, were located. At such places as Bloedel, Rock Bay, Sayward, Englewood; and later at Beaver Cove, regions, the expansion of year-round housing provided for permanent logging settlements, which were slowly linked by logging roads to Campbell River or to neighbouring communities. As a result the rush of entire logging crews to reach the big city by ship on the twice-yearly shutdowns was greatly reduced.

On 22 August 1927, Capt. Andy Johnstone, in command of the *Cardena,* skillfully saved the Canadian National liner *Prince Rupert* from almost certain disaster in the treacherous Seymour Narrows. Southbound, and within 10 hours of Vancouver, he heard distress signals ahead in the narrows. A sudden lift of the mist revealed the *Prince Rupert* hard aground, "pronged" on Ripple Rock and helpless with her rudder locked.

Captain Johnstone eased the *Cardena* as close alongside as he dared and had a steel towing line cast aboard the liner which was made fast to her stern. Incredibly, with sharp, sudden tugs he pulled the *Prince Rupert* clear of the reef and towed the almost unmanageable ship two miles into Deep Bay where he took off all the passengers he could accommodate and signalled for help. Johnstone received high commendation from the company and from Canadian National for his magnificent rescue feat.

The Union almost lost its new *Catala* on 8 November 1927, when, after leaving Port Simpson, she took the shorter Cunningham Passage to Prince Rupert and ran heavily aground off Mist Island. She became stranded on an outcrop of the same reef marked on the other side of the channel by the Sparrowhawk buoy where a British light cruiser had been wrecked. Boats were lowered to take off the 44 passengers, all of whom were transferred to a tug and Indian launches and taken to Port Simpson. The accident occurred at almost high tide. Low tide disclosed that, although the ship was not taking water, her hull was cradled at a dangerous angle, high and dry between two sharp pinnacles of the reef.

First efforts to free her failed, but the splendid work of Pacific Salvage in building a coffer dam, and patching the hull temporarily, refloated the *Catala* before winter storms could damage her. Under the supervision of W.D. McLaren, her original builder, the staunch *Catala* was restored at Burrard Drydock at a cost of $175,000 and rejoined the fleet in March.

In Vancouver harbour, the departure of five Union day vessels on Saturday afternoons was one of the exciting events. The *Lady Alexandra,* or the "Alec" as she was fondly known, often carried capacity excursion loads, especially inbound from Bowen Island on Sunday evenings. The number of picnic fields, all with covered tables, had now been increased to six and nearly all were in use on Wednesdays, weekends, and holidays. The opening of the large pavilion, for shelter and dancing, often saved the day when showers interfered with picnic sports.

Moonlight Cruises to the island resort, with dancing on board the *Lady Alexandra,* were held on Wednesday and Saturday nights and became one of Vancouverites' popular summer outings from the mid-1920s. A Vancouver orchestra provided music for the twice-weekly dances at the Bowen pavilion.

Band concerts, special public sports programs, and Frank Scott's vaudeville at the Bowen shell were featured on many weekends. Employees of large companies, such as the Hudson's Bay Company, B.C. Electric, Woodward's, Spencer's, and B.C. Telephone, chartered the *Lady Alexandra* for outings. It was a busy three months for the day vessels. The Union provided 3,000 excursions without mishap.

On 27 July 1929, after the departure of Saturday-afternoon steamers, fire destroyed a large part of the Union wharf shed, but the berthed ships were towed to safety. The adjoining Pier H was leased for the Union's northern sailings and cargo-ship loadings for several months. The construction of a much larger Union shed, with improved facilities and more storage space, began almost immediately.

That summer the company lost Chairman Grange V. Holt, the well-known banker, who was killed in a traffic accident. He was succeeded by R. Kerr Houlgate, a prominent Vancouver insurance executive and a former president of the Vancouver Board of Trade.

The Depression cut coastal trade and the export market. The general slump did not, fortunately, greatly affect the popularity of Bowen Island or the low-priced excursions. Harold Brown managed to hold the Union family together, despite two salary cuts through the office and shore staff.

The company lost two of its Welsford principals in 1930. The sudden death of Sir Arnold Rushton on 5 February snapped a familiar link with the Liverpool head office since 1911. Apart from his shipping responsibilities, he played a strenuous role in public affairs. His death preceded by only three months that of Major George B. Haddock, Welsford's chairman, a prominent Union shareholder and one-time partner of the founder.

General Manager Harold Brown was forced to impose operating economies, but although the fishing and mining business had suffered, the northern routes began to improve and the excursion vessels enjoyed a bumper season in 1931. As was his custom, President Richard Welsford had spent the summer in Vancouver when he suddenly fell ill and died. He was only 35. Although lacking the drive of his father, he had initiated the greatest ship expansion of the Union line.

On 31 October 1931, the J.H. Welsford & Co. Ltd. in Liverpool wound up voluntarily. The Welsford family still held a controlling interest in the Union Steamship Company, but Harold Brown, now the managing director, stressed in his Christmas message that, operationally, the Union line was a B.C. company and would become even more local in character. However, the lack of fresh capital, and the need to protect the large British investment, meant that risks had to be avoided, especially costly ship replacements. So he tried to maintain the existing service by rebuilding older vessels like the *Cheakamus* and the *Chilco*. The latter was converted with day-boat furnishings and a modern saloon in 1935 and renamed the *Lady Pam* in honour of Mrs. Brown.

A bonus in the 1930s was the popularity of new excursions. The *Lady Alexandra* featured Fraser River trips to New Westminster, with passengers being returned to Vancouver by bus. In August 1931 a trip was sponsored by the Surrey Legion from the White Rock pier to Victoria and other day trips from White Rock were made until 1939. These excursions to Victoria carried the maximum 900 passengers. The most popular excursion was the all-day sail of 160 miles to Savary Island and return, with a call at Powell River. Tried as an experiment in 1933 at the bargain price of $2, and limited to 450 passengers, two trips were run weekly with full loads for seven seasons, a total of 172. The fare never bus. In August 1931 a trip was sponsored by the Surrey speed of 15 1/2 knots by the *Lady Cynthia* or the *Lady Cecilia,* with all meals available on board.

Although the scheduled passenger business to the north soon recovered, the bulk-freighting of the *Chilkoot* and the

Chilliwack suffered from competition from the Frank Waterhouse vessels and independent tramps. The major oil companies and fish packers were also using their own tankers and supply vessels along the coast. Consequently one of the company's freighters had to be laid up on occasion. The *Chilkoot* was sold in 1934 for much below her value, but despite the economic difficulties it was a bad decision, particularly as the sale did not prevent her adding to the competition. During the next decade, after being dieselized, this fine cargo vessel ran against her former Union sister ships.

The older ships *Camosun* and *Lady Evelyn* were retired in 1936. Plans for a new northern steamer were postponed, and eventually shelved, because of the high cost of construction. The only new vessel ordered was the 105.0′ motor ship *Lady Sylvia,* which was launched on the Clyde and sailed for Vancouver on 7 May 1937 from Glasgow under Capt. W.E. Smailes with a crew of only nine. She encountered stormy weather twice on her Atlantic crossing, and coming up the Pacific coast battled mountainous seas for seven days before reaching Vancouver on 10 July. Designed for West Howe Sound service, and off-season relief, she was renamed the *Lady Rose* when a registry duplication was discovered.

The Union Steamship Company returned to British Columbia ownership on 1 August 1937, after a Vancouver business group, represented by M.J.K. Allen and E.F. Buckerfield, bought the Welsford family's controlling shares. The quoted figure of about $1 million was barely a third of the price that had been asked in secret talks with Canadian National Steamships in 1928. A report of CNS negotiations published in *Fairplay,* a British shipping journal,

had been denied by the Union's chairman. The truth was that the bid had been made directly to the Welsford company, and for secrecy and mutual convenience, Richard Welsford had gone to New York to meet with CN representatives. The negotiations broke down, but there is little doubt that the B.C. coast came within an ace of having a line of federal ships serving its ports. A few months later Sir Henry Thornton announced the laying down of three CN luxury liners for the B.C. coast.

By 1937 the Union fleet was showing its age and need for major replacements. First announcements by the new British Columbia owners were optimistic, but were followed by the decision to defer building new ships because of prohibitive costs. Harold Brown was appointed president. J.K. Macrae, K.C., who became chairman in 1936 after the death of R. Kerr Houlgate that year, continued in office until 1943. Extensive renovations on the fleet continued in 1938, and included valuable improvements to the *Chelohsin's* accommodations.

In March 1938 Carl Halterman, a local shipping man prominent in the grain trade, was appointed assistant general manager, and became general manager in February 1939, with President Harold Brown retaining policy direction.

In September 1938 the company bought 50 acres of property containing a tearoom and several cottages at Whytecliff, overlooking Howe Sound, for its Union Estates division. The move had the dual purpose of creating a scenic and convenient dining resort and providing the logical site and parking area for a second and auxiliary ferry crossing to Snug Cove, Bowen Island. The M.V. *Comox,* which had served on this crossing in 1924, was put back into this service along with a smaller launch and carried 10,000 passengers in the first season. The Cliff House restaurant provided luncheons, as well as dinners with music and dancing.

The Union celebrated its Golden Jubilee in the summer of 1939, an event coinciding with the visit to Vancouver of King George VI and Queen Elizabeth. Union day ships brought 4,000 settlers and school children from coast communities on special excursions, and the larger vessels were used for sightseeing in the harbour. When the royal party left for Victoria on 29 May, the destroyer escort was followed by six Union ships with 2,500 aboard.

In September 1939 the lights went out along the B.C. coast following Canada's declaration of war against Germany. Ship operations were carried out in blackness, except for navigation lights. This wartime measure made piloting through narrow waterways to small landings very difficult and dangerous and was possible only because of long experience and a friendly lantern at the last moment. Ports were blacked out and other security measures imposed, such as girding the vessels' hulls with degaussing cables and trailing paravanes—"the spinning tops"—to divert enemy mines in the steamers' track.

Upon America's entry into the war in December 1941, the North Pacific became a vital war zone. The ships' navigating bridges were armoured and stern guns installed and manned by trained naval gunners. Even the distribution of printed sailing schedules was restricted because the Union's routes to the north were used for transport of service personnel and supplies. Foodstuffs and vital materials were delivered to the Pacific war stations at Yorke Island, Port Hardy, Bella Bella, Prince Rupert, and Sandspit (the air base in the Queen Charlotte Islands). The B.C. coast was now in "the front line" with Canadian naval patrols on the alert for Japanese submarines prowling off Hecate Strait and the shores of Vancouver Island, and guarding the entrance to the inside passage to the north.

Two months after the outbreak of war, the Union bought the cargo fleet of Frank Waterhouse & Company of Canada Ltd., comprising the 20-year-old freighters *Northholm, Southholm,* and *Eastholm,* as well as two chartered vessels, the *Gray* and the *Bervin* (the company's old *Coquitlam*). The Union-Waterhouse Cargo Division was then formed with the former Waterhouse manager, R.L. Solloway, in charge. Their office staff and personnel were moved to the Union pier and allotted a section of the Union's head office. The cargo division's vessels, including the freighter *Chilliwack,* continued to operate until 1955 under the Waterhouse colours: a black funnel with a "W" on a star in a white circle.

The combined fleet now comprised 11 passenger-freighters and 6 cargo vessels, grossing 13,500 tons, under the general and administrative control of Carl Halterman. After serving as traffic and personal assistant to the general manager since 1925, I was appointed traffic manager for the passenger ships. The Union's sailing schedules from this date included a section listing the Union-Waterhouse cargo routes and operations. It would be more than five years before the Union could resume normal schedules and carry out the full reconditioning overhaul of every ship.

1919-1939

The Union Fleet in Photographs

CAPILANO II
CARDENA
CATALA
CHEAM
CHILKOOT I
CHILLIWACK I
CHILLIWACK II
COMOX II
EASTHOLM
GRAY
LADY ALEXANDRA
LADY CECILIA
LADY CYNTHIA
LADY EVELYN
LADY ROSE
NORTHHOLM
SOUTHHOLM

1 *Harold Brown, president of the Union company from 1938 to 1943. Pictures on wall show (left to right) Ernest Beazley, Grange V. Holt, R. Kerr Houlgate and Sir Arnold Rushton.*

2 *The* Chilliwack, *loaded with canned salmon, entering Vancouver harbour, about 1921.*

3 *The* Chilliwack *off the Union dock.*

4 *The freighter* Chilkoot *entering Burrard Inlet, heavily loaded with salmon.*

5 *The freighter* Chilkoot *headed for the Union pier.*

2

3

4

5

6 *The large upper deck and graceful lines of the* Capilano *can be seen in this photograph. She was built to serve the Selma Park resort and gulf coast summer trade.*

7 *The* Capilano *homeward bound to Vancouver rounding Gower Point.*

8 *The* Capilano's *comfortable main-deck saloon gave entrance to a 36-seat dining room.*

6

7

8

9 *The* Cheam *in Snug Cove, Bowen Island. As the* Bowena *she had already carried many picnickers.*

10 *The* Bowena *at the Bowen Island wharf landing a party of picnickers.*

11 *The* Cheam *en route to Howe Sound.*

12 *The* Bowena *under Terminal Steam Navigation colours, with Howe Sound excursionists. She would become the Union's* Cheam.

9

10

11

12

BOWEN ISLAND

T HIS BEAUTIFUL RESORT is reached after ONE HOUR'S pleasant sail from Vancouver on our fast and commodious steamers. The Company's estate, known as "Bowen Park," is now continentally popular. Some of the outstanding attractions are pictorially featured in the following pages, and great improvements have been planned for the benefit of visitors during the coming season.

Last year the fine new dance hall was completed, and this year a wonderful salt-water swimming pool, with sand bottom, will be ready for use in the lagoon.

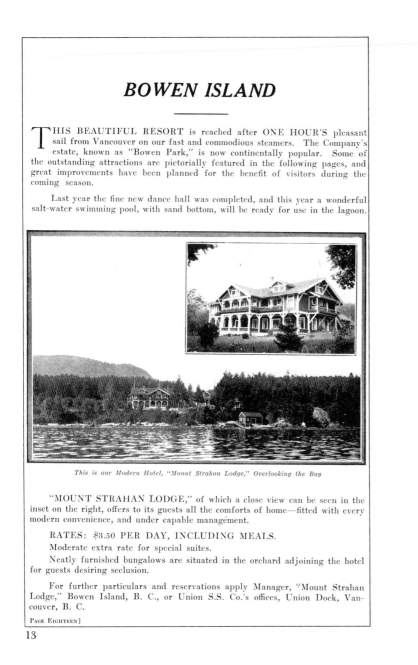

This is our Modern Hotel, "Mount Strahan Lodge," Overlooking the Bay

"MOUNT STRAHAN LODGE," of which a close view can be seen in the inset on the right, offers to its guests all the comforts of home—fitted with every modern convenience, and under capable management.

RATES: $3.50 PER DAY, INCLUDING MEALS.

Moderate extra rate for special suites.

Neatly furnished bungalows are situated in the orchard adjoining the hotel for guests desiring seclusion.

For further particulars and reservations apply Manager, "Mount Strahan Lodge," Bowen Island, B. C., or Union S.S. Co.'s offices, Union Dock, Vancouver, B. C.

PAGE EIGHTEEN]

13

Where to Spend Your Picnic !

The Happy Throng on the Wharf to Greet the Arriving Picnic Party

ONE THOUSAND ACRES is maintained by the Company for the picnicker. Plenty of hot water and picnic tables adjoin Nos. 1, 2 and 3 grounds. Refreshments required can be purchased at stores close at hand at practically city prices.

"The Children's Race."

Special arrangements and terms made for picnic parties.

Apply to the Head Office, Union S.S. Co., in Vancouver, and reserve your picnic date in time.

View of our No. 1 Ground, with a picnic party enjoying themselves.

PAGE TWENTY]

Special Evening
Dances Arranged
Throughout the
Season

Good Orchestra
and
Polished Spring
Floor

The New Modern Dance Hall, Bowen Park

This magnificent pavilion, the largest in British Columbia, was completed in 1921, and is capable of dancing 800 couples.

The building is planned on octagonal lines, and, with a circular floor and central raised dais for bandstand, is very imposing, and placed amid delightful surroundings.

Bathing and boating are among the many recreations available

A New Salt-water Swimming Pool is Ready for this Season

Swimming sports may be held in perfect safety, with every convenience. The pool will be of regulation size, properly banked and fitted out; it will also have a graded sand bottom, and can be used by both SWIMMERS AND NON-SWIMMERS!

Bathing from the gently sloping beach is also popular.

BOATING in the bay and nearby waters is delightful. There are two boat-houses, from either of which boats may be hired at reasonable rates.

EXCURSION PARTIES can also be arranged with the management.

[PAGE TWENTY-ONE

14

15

16

17 *The "little tots" race.*

18 *Ladies' race at an early Bowen Island*
picnic on No. 1 grounds.

19 *Games and sports attracted day-trippers*
to Bowen Park's picnic grounds. The
men's flat race on No. 1 grounds
alongside the main bathing beach.

17

18

19

20. *A picnic at Bowen Island, circa 1917.*

21 *Later the Union company built covered tables, which provided ample seating and shelter, on six separate grounds.*

20

21

22 *The* Lady Evelyn *was a popular early excursion vessel.*

23 *The* Lady Evelyn *in West Howe Sound.*

24 *The* Lady Evelyn *at Gibsons.*

22

23

24

27 *The S.S.* **Cardena** *saves the disabled Canadian National S.S.* **Prince Rupert** *by pulling her off Ripple Rock, Seymour Narrows, where she was impaled on 22 August 1927—a magnificent feat by Capt. Andrew Johnstone.*

28 *Transfer of passengers from the* **Prince Rupert.**

27

28

29 *The M.V.* Comox *ran a ferry service
in 1924 and again in 1940 between
Whytecliff float and Snug Cove, Bowen
Island. Seen here coming to the rescue
of an overturned craft.*

31 *Vancouver's excursion queen, the* Lady
   Alexandra. *From her arrival in 1924
   until after World War II she carried
   3,000 public and charter excursions.*

31

32 *Boarding the* Lady Alexandra *for a "show-boat" cruise with Theatre Under the Stars' entertainers. TUTS' group included Lorraine McAllister (third from left), Flora Anders (third from right), and (end, face partly hidden) Betty Phillips.*

33 *The Woodward's annual staff picnic aboard the* Lady Alexandra.

32

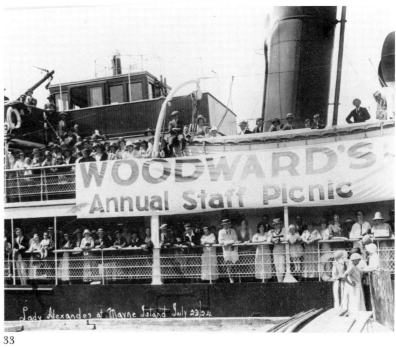

33

34 *On the bridge of the* Lady Alexandra
*for the company's 60th jubilee picnic:
(left to right) E.G. Eakins, personnel
manager; John Gilligan, assistant chief
engineer; Capt. William L. Yates;
Capt. E.W. Suffield, marine
superintendent; the author.*

35 *The* Lady Alexandra *shown alongside Bowen Island wharf in beautiful Snug Cove.*

36 *The* Lady Alexandra, *excursion flags flying, leads a Saturday picnic fleet to Bowen Island.*

37 *Passengers disembarking from the* Lady Alexandra *at the Bowen Island wharf.*

35

36

37

38 *The* Lady Alexandra *leaving Selma Park in 1925 with a charter picnic group of perhaps 1,200.*

39 *The* Lady Alexandra's *dining saloon, easily convertible for dancing.*

38

39

41 *Luncheon menu served on board the* Cardena, *1 August 1934, and Christmas dinner menu of the* S.S. Camosun, *1954.*

TRIPS BY UNION SHIPS ARE PLEASANT, RESTFUL, RECREATIVE

LUNCHEON menu — UNION ESTAB'D STEAMSHIPS

On Board "CARDENA"   E. GEORGESON   Master

Aug. 1st.

RELISHES
Sardines on Toast   Iced Queen Olives

SOUPS
Barley Broth   Consomme

FISH
Boiled Ling Cod Parsley Sauce

SALAD
Tomato Mayonnaise

ENTREES
Boiled Ox Heart Italian Sauce
Veal Fricassee & Green Peas
Banana Fritter Maple Syrup

JOINTS
Roast Prime Ribs of Beef & Horseradish
Roast Leg of Mutton Currant Jelly

VEGETABLES
Steamed Potatoes   Mashed Potatoes
String Beans

DESSERT
Steamed Marmalade Pudding Sweet Sauce
Green Apple Pie   Pear Pie
Raspberry Jelly with Whipped Cream
Vanilla Ice Cream   Plain & Fruit Cake

CHEESE
Canadian Stilton   Roquefort
MacLaren's   Kraft

Tea   Milk   Buttermilk   Coffee
Fresh Fruit   Mixed Nuts

S. S. "Camosun"   UNION STEAMSHIPS   E. McQuarrie
On Board   Chief Engineer
J. J. Halcrow   C. A. Anderson
Master   Purser
Dec. 25th, 1954.   N. Davidson
Date   Chief Steward

X M A S   D I N N E R

Stuffed Celery   Gherkins   Ripe Olives
Silver Onions   Crabmeat Cocktail

Chicken Noodle Soup

Poached Fillet of Halibut, Hollandaise

Chicken Salad, Mayonnaise

Baked Virginia Ham, Slice Pineapple
Saute of Fresh Mushrooms with Bacon

Roast Stuffed Tom Turkey, Cranberry Sauce
Roast Prime Ribs of Beef, Yorkshire Pudding

Steamed or Mashed Potatoes
Brussel Sprouts   Green Peas

Steamed Plum Pudding, Hard Sauce
Hot or Cold Mince Pie   Lemon Tarts
Wine Jello, Whipped Cream
Vanilla Ice Cream   Xmas Cake

Canadian Cheddar or McLarens Cheese

Mixed Nuts   Fresh Fruit

Tea   Milk   Buttermilk   Coffee

Union Steamships wish all patrons
A Merry Christmas
A Happy New Year

42 *The* Lady Cecilia *loaded with excursionists to Sechelt and the gulf coast.*

43 *The* Lady Cecilia: *covered alleyways with observation windows.*

44 *The* Lady Cecilia: *upper passenger deck.*

42

43

44

45 *The* Lady Cecilia: *forward observation lounge.*

46 *The* Lady Cecilia: *dining room.*

45

46

47 *The* Lady Cynthia *outward bound on a holiday excursion.*

48 *The* Lady Cynthia *passing Stanley Park en route to Vancouver harbour. Structural improvements in 1940 caused one of her funnels to be removed.*

49 *The* Lady Cynthia *at Snug Cove wharf, Bowen Island.*

47

48

49

50 *The* Catala *with her large promenade deck had the appearance of a liner.*

51 *The* Catala *at Bella Bella, a regular call on her weekly route to Prince Rupert and Stewart.*

52 *The* Catala *impaled on a reef south of Port Simpson, 8 November 1927. The vessel was recovered and partly rebuilt.*

50

51

52

53 *The* Lady Rose *was requisitioned in 1942 for naval transport service on the west coast of Vancouver Island and served in that capacity until 1946.*

54 *The* Lady Rose, *launched and completed under the name* Lady Sylvia *at the Pointhouse Shipyard in Glasgow, was the smallest of the Union's day steamers.*

55 *The* Lady Rose *calls at Bowen Island on her route to West Howe Sound. The small motor ferry* Bowen *is alongside the dock.*

53

54

55

56 *The strong cargo ship* Chilliwack II, *bought at Glasgow, was well suited to B.C.'s coastal needs. She had a 60' forward hatch, fish oil tanks, and capacity to stow 28,000 cases of canned salmon.*

57 *The* Gray, *once a competitor on the northern routes, was purchased by the Union company from Waterhouse Company and became a useful wartime freighter.*

58 *The* Northholm, *showing the Waterhouse Company funnel (which was also carried by other cargo division vessels of the period), foundered off the north tip of Vancouver Island in a gale, 16 January 1943.*

56

57

58

59 *The* Southholm, *one of the larger*
    Union-Waterhouse freighters, operated
    to Englewood, Alert Bay, and beyond.

59

60 *The* Southholm *in a coastal port.*

61 *The* Southholm *converted to the company's* Bulk Carrier No. 1 *in 1950.*

62 *The* Eastholm, *smallest of the Waterhouse freighters, regularly served Texada Island and the gulf coast.*

60

61

62

63 *The* Eastholm *alongside the Evans Coleman pier, Vancouver.*

64 *The* Eastholm, *with her shallow-draft wooden hull, was a handy vessel for local and Puget Sound service.*

63

64

65 *Six Union ships returning from a Howe Sound "War Savings" cruise on 29 July 1940. Capt. John Muir, superintendent, led the marine parade in the* Lady Cynthia, *under Capt. H.E. Lawrey.*

65

66 *The west side of the Union pier in 1924, looking across the harbour to Vancouver's north shore. Shows six Union vessels and visiting battle cruiser H.M.S. Hood in background.*

1940-1959

Post-War Struggle; The Whistle is Silent

I am still in love with the memory of the
gallant little craft that plied the stormy B.C.
waters bringing food and equipment and
gossip to so many far-flung spots of isolated
beauty. . . . The old Union boats were part of
the warp and woof of British Columbia of
long ago.

—Fred Lindsay,
B.C. journalist

In 1940, top-level meetings were initiated by the Canadian
National Steamships with the Union's General Manager Carl
Halterman to discuss combining or meshing the northern
schedules of both lines for mutual economy in the wartime
emergency. The result was that on 8 June the Union
announced it had taken over the federally subsidized service
to the Queen Charlotte Islands and had purchased two older
ships of the Canadian National fleet—the *Prince Charles* and
the *Prince John,* then engaged on this route from Vancouver via
Prince Rupert.

The *Prince Charles,* launched in 1907 as the *St. Margaret* and
licensed for 150 passengers to the Charlottes, was renamed
the *Camosun II.* The *Prince John,* built in 1910 but licensed for
only 85 passengers from Prince Rupert, had a cargo capacity
of 400 tons. She was given another proud Union name:
Cassiar II.

The QCI route had not been profitable, despite federal
subsidization, but because of the war the lumber camps were
working at full capacity. Moreover, the heavy volume of cargo
and personnel needed by the air base at Alliford Bay in
Skidegate Inlet warranted the added Union freight and
passenger accommodation.

Another recipient of the Union's service was the Aero
Timber Company, which operated five locomotives on 20
miles of track at Cumshewa Inlet in the south Charlotte
island. Aero, the former Allison Logging Company, had been
bought by the federal government to assure the production of
airplane spruce—a war priority.

To assist the homefront war effort, short cruises were begun
in July 1940 with free passage for buyers of war savings
stamps. Overnight pleasure travel was curtailed because of
wartime priorities on cabin space, and thousands of
holidayers turned to day excursions for relaxation. On one
occasion, about 3,000 people embarked from Vancouver for
an evening cruise on seven Union ships. Gasoline rationing
also contributed to the number of boat-trippers. The *Catala,
Cardena, Chelohsin,* and *Venture,* which provided berths for
service personnel bound for defence points, were taxed to the
limit. Arrivals of Union ships at upcoast ports, particularly
after the blackout was imposed in 1939, were special events
for residents of the many small communities who were
virtually cut off from the outside world by the critical events
of the war in 1941.

With marine radios silenced and steamer arrival times
unpredictable, owners of small boats and "Mission vessels"
often faced hazardous trips from small camps or settlements
to the nearest hospital centres when the seriously ill or
injured required emergency treatment. Amazing rescues were
performed using only crude marine aids to help cross the
open Milbanke Sound or Queen Charlotte Sound in dead of
night. When a Union vessel was expected, a local wharfinger
often slept on or near the wharf or a landing float to flash a
lantern at a crucial moment for the Union ship bringing the
weekly supplies and mail. Often a barking dog was the best
direction finder for an approaching ship.

Mrs. Clyde W. (Nancy) Gildersleeve, of the well-known coast logging family, who helped her husband to operate the camp boat and then a mission craft, wrote:

> We learned navigation the hard way during the blackout years, when we so often had to take sick and injured loggers on the 11-hour trip (it always seemed to be at night) from Smith's Inlet to Bella Bella, where they were put under Dr. George E. Darby's skilful care.
>
> The only navigational aids we had were a compass and some old charts. Crossing Queen Charlotte Sound without the lights of the lighthouses and blinkers was something . . . with radio silence it was anybody's guess when the Union boat would arrive. Sometimes we waited two days at Margaret Bay, near where the camp was then situated. It seemed that she always came in at the most unearthly hours, generally between 2 A.M. and 4 A.M. We would hear the familiar "long, two shorts, and a long" whistle and turn out of warm sleeping bags into the cold night. Our initial grumpiness was soon dispelled by the cheery service of the officers and crew, who also had to be out in the wind, rain, snow, or whatever.
>
> There was a saying around the coast that the Union boats would stop anywhere for a man in a rowboat who wanted to post a letter and buy two bits worth of stamps. And they did, too!

In 1941, the Canadian Pacific Railway, through its Consolidated Mining & Smelting Company, bought a controlling interest in the Union Steamship Company of B.C. Ltd. For a time this change in ownership was known only to the chief operating personnel. T.W. Bingay, general manager of Cominco at Trail, joined the Union board, but there was no interference with the company's normal operations nor any outward change.

The *Lady Rose,* which had been transporting artillery personnel and supplies to Yorke Island fort at the head of Johnstone Strait, was requisitioned by the government for naval and air force transport service on the west coast of Vancouver Island.

The *Camosun* and the *Cassiar* were working to capacity over the next three years carrying loggers and supplies from Vancouver and Prince Rupert to the Queen Charlotte Islands, and increasing numbers of service personnel to Alliford Bay. The *Camosun* departures direct to the south Charlottes were on an increased frequency every 10 days, carrying loggers to Aero Timber, Morgan's, and Kelley's camps in Cumshewa Inlet, then via Skidegate Inlet to the Pacific Mills camp at Sandspit and via Masset Inlet to Prince Rupert. The *Cassiar* alternated with sailings via the Inside Passage, loading more cargo and passengers at Prince Rupert for the Queen Charlottes. A Union-Waterhouse vessel with heavier cargo also crossed to the Charlottes occasionally.

After the United States entered the war in December 1941, the Union-Waterhouse division was engaged in emergency cargo transport to the north and performed special contracts for the U.S. Department of Transport. In 1942 the *Cheakamus* was converted into a towboat and another hull was purchased for conversion to the barge *Commando* to carry urgent war cargoes. The *Cheakamus* later was sold to the American government as a salvage tug.

Movements north on the *Cardena* and *Catala* were now so demanding that the *Chelohsin* was assigned to a twice-weekly schedule as far as Port Hardy. She relieved those two ships of lower-end calls at Englewood, Alert Bay, and Port McNeill, and also took over the transport of men and supplies for the

Port Hardy air base and of loggers for Quatsino Sound. Port Hardy, with Tex Lyons as the Union agent and wharfinger, was the passenger connecting point for Port Alice and the west coast. It was a key post for Lyons at this stage of the war.

Simultaneously, the Waterhouse cargo ships under Solloway's direction were engaged in a gigantic build-up of supplies at the new American Forces assembly base at Port Edward near Prince Rupert. The population of Prince Rupert increased to over 12,000 during the next two years as American transports called there on their way to the war zone. In one defence move, the *Cardena* picked up a complete RCAF squadron at Sidney, Vancouver Island, and landed it at the Annette Island base in U.S. Alaskan waters.

President Harold Brown retired at the end of 1942 and moved to Victoria. He was succeeded by Gordon Farrell, well-known industrialist and senior officer of the B.C. Telephone Co., who had served on the Union board since 1929. F.H. Clendenning and J.S. Eckman became vice-presidents and Carl Halterman was appointed managing director. Gerald McBean, who came to the Union as assistant manager in 1941 after heading the Canadian Transport Company, was now co-ordinating the expanding Waterhouse cargo division with the Union's six passenger routes.

On 16 January 1943, the Waterhouse freighter *Northholm*, which had left Port Alice with a full load of pulp, foundered in a raging gale off Cape Scott, Vancouver Island, with the loss of Capt. F. McMahon and 14 of his crew of 17. The first news of the tragedy reached Vancouver three days later by telephone from a trapper, who had found Chief Officer Ray Perry and seaman A.H. Gerbrandt, sole survivors from the only lifeboat that could be launched.

The husky Perry, a Newfoundlander born to the sea, kept his lifeboat afloat in sight of land in the heavy seas until the storm had abated near dusk, when he managed to get a sail hoisted. It was hours after midnight before the lifeboat reached the beach, and six crewmen had died from exposure to the freezing weather before he and Gerbrandt struggled ashore. At daybreak they were quickly spotted and were picked up two days later.

With long-distance sea travel still under restriction, outings for the one-hour sail to the convenient Bowen Park resort continued to be popular with Vancouverites. The Moonlight Dance Cruise also drew hundreds of boat-trippers, and the *Lady Alexandra* was strictly patrolled on the late sailing at this period to ensure orderliness as the passengers sought relief from wartime tensions.

The revenue of the Union Steamship Company reached an all-time high in 1943, but wartime profits taxes drained off most of it. Because of the greatly increased costs of operating and maintaining the older ships, the long-term outlook was not too optimistic for the company.

Selma Park was sold by Union Estates in 1944 to private interests. Its importance to the company as a resort and picnic centre had diminished with the improvements and growth of nearby Sechelt on the gulf coast. That year the 165.0' motor vessel *Island King,* with a cargo capacity of 800 tons, was bought for the Union-Waterhouse service, and placed on a weekly freight route to Port Alice via Quatsino Sound ports, returning with full loads of pulp.

Gerald McBean took over as general manager in 1945 from Carl Halterman, who became vice-president of operations. At war's end McBean took up with the Canadian Maritime Commission the urgent matter of lifting the freeze on coastal freight and passenger rates, which had been controlled since 1939. A welcome revision was granted, but not enough to offset the increased costs of fuel oil, insurance, longshoring, and maintenance repairs, all of which combined had risen

130 per cent in wartime and were never to come down.

Harold Brown died in 1945 at Victoria. He was highly regarded in the fleet and in business circles, especially the Vancouver Board of Trade, as well as in the upcoast communities where he created much goodwill during the 15 years that he presided over the Union's fortunes. His genius for travel promotion ushered in the British Columbia coast's tourist and excursion bonanza.

By war's end, the Union's passenger fleet was run down after missing the husbanding and reconditioning of normal times, and new vessels were urgently needed. With logging activity and work crews in the Queen Charlottes reduced by two-thirds, and the removal of the entire RCAF base and stores from Alliford Bay, the *Camosun II* was withdrawn and sold in September 1945. The venerable *Venture* was also sold the following year to Chinese buyers. With the return of the *Lady Rose* from government transport service, the *Lady Pam* was retired.

As a first move towards replacement tonnage, Carl Halterman took over a China-coaster-type freighter being built at Victoria Machinery Depot. This 214.0′ vessel was christened the *Chilkoot II* on 26 June 1946 and put into Union-Waterhouse service to relieve the smaller *Island King* on the weekly pulp route to Port Alice.

A major decision was made in the fall of 1945 to speedily obtain northern passenger replacements, if only to serve for an interim period. Three surplus Castle-class corvettes were bought for $75,000 each from the War Assets Corporation for conversion to coastal-service ships. The estimated cost of conversion to enable more than 100 first-class passengers to be carried in excellent accommodations, and 250 tons of cargo, was about $500,000 each. Two of the ships were intended for northern routes; the third was planned for Alaska cruises but with facilities similar to those of the others for relief service. The first new ship was expected to be in service by the late summer of 1946.

Contracts for the conversion of two of the corvettes to the new *Coquitlam II* and the *Chilcotin* were placed with West Coast Shipbuilders under the supervision of W.D. McLaren, the Union's former builder at Montrose and now well established in British Columbia. The contract for conversion of the third corvette to the *Camosun III* was given to Burrard Drydock Company, also long associated with the Union line.

The plans provided for a new standard of passenger accommodation. The entire 26 upper-deck rooms, about half the total cabins, were to be finished as deluxe staterooms with private showers and toilets. Four of these rooms were to be fitted with either twin beds or bathtubs, and all were to have hot and cold running water, fold-away berths, and settees. Maximum safety features to be provided included radar, depth sounder, bow rudder, and transmission steering, with wireless telegraph and radio equipment.

Vice-President Carl Halterman announced a further purchase in August 1946 of four Bangor minesweepers, 50.0′ shorter and considerably smaller than the corvettes, which were to be converted for coast service with diesel engines at a cost of $200,000 each. Three of them were intended for day-steamer replacements, superior to Gulf Lines' small vessels then competing along the Powell River route, and the fourth was an overnight cabin vessel for the logging route. However, with greatly increased costs for the corvette conversions now in progress, and an abrupt drop in local travel, the second project was scrapped and the Bangors were sold. Except possibly for the selling of the Bangor that was to have been converted to an overnight vessel, this was a wise decision in the light of later events.

Completion of the first corvette conversion was three months later than scheduled due to technical and other factors that could hardly have been foreseen. Had the company known that none of the new ships could be put into profitable use before the 1947 season, a second look might well have been given to the project.

The new *Coquitlam II* sailed on 8 November 1946 under Capt. John Boden for Prince Rupert and Stewart; a month later the *Camosun* left under Capt. Ernest Sheppard for Ocean Falls, Prince Rupert, and Ketchikan—the first regular Alaskan passenger call by a Union ship in more than 40 years.

Completed with special cruise features, the *Chilcotin* sailed for Prince Rupert with a convention party on 21 May 1947 under Capt. A.C. McLennan. In June she began a new weekly cruise to Ketchikan via the spectacular Gardner Canal and Prince Rupert, with sightseeing calls en route. The trips were sold to capacity for three summers, thus more than fulfilling Gerald McBean's expectations for this phase of the conversion project. In 1951 the cruise was extended from six to ten days to include Juneau and Skagway, where a stopover offered the choice of a memorable White Pass & Yukon rail trip to Lake Bennett, to the West Taku Arm, or to Whitehorse. The call at Sitka was later cancelled in favour of a magnificent cruise through Glacier Bay. Tour parties came from all over the United States. Such was the popularity of the *Chilcotin* (she was sold out every season) that in travel circles her name became synonymous with Alaskan cruises.

All three new ships made money in the tourist season, but lost heavily the rest of the year when their operating costs far exceeded those of specially designed, economical earlier ships. In the fall of 1947 the *Camosun* was tried on an extended route to Petersburg and Wrangell, but was soon withdrawn. In December, Gerald McBean announced plans to withdraw these three vessels for the winter, but in response to strong northern protests the *Coquitlam II* was put on a 10-day route to the Queen Charlottes via Prince Rupert. The *Cardena* and the *Catala* were assigned to other winter routes. With these changes, the outlook slowly improved, and losses were curtailed by more economical schedules. McBean, now the managing director, obtained additional subsidization of the northern operations.

The Diamond Jubilee of the Union Steamship Company was celebrated in June 1949 with a week of bargain excursions, including "show-boat" cruises with Vancouver's Theatre Under the Stars performers and musicians playing aboard the *Lady Alexandra*. However, because new roads and ferries provided a convenient link via Horseshoe Bay to the Sechelt Peninsula, local day service was reduced. This decline ultimately forced the withdrawal of the Union's day steamers, which had contributed so greatly to building up the Sunshine Coast resorts. After serving this area since 1920, the *Capilano* was retired in 1950, and the *Lady Cecilia* was sold the following year.

A crippling blow that hastened the withdrawal of older excursion vessels hit shipping companies on both coasts on 17 September 1949 when the *Noronic,* a large Great Lakes vessel, was gutted by fire in Toronto harbour with a loss of 119 lives. Stringent new marine fire regulations were introduced for all coast vessels, and made mandatory sprinkler systems and clocked fire stations with hourly patrols. The installation cost for the Union's day ships alone was $250,000. After 1952, the *Lady Alexandra* was used only for a limited season and that left only one day steamer, the *Lady Cynthia,* serving the Bowen Island-Squamish route.

The *Cassiar II,* which had provided wartime service to the Queen Charlottes, was retired in 1949. Despite the *Chelohsin's* age, it was a regrettable loss when this pioneer and still serviceable ship was stranded in fog on the night of 6 November 1949 outside Vancouver harbour close to Siwash Rock, off Stanley Park. Fifty-three passengers were rowed ashore. After several attempts to salvage her, she was abandoned to the underwriters. Although the wreck was recovered, this was the end of a grand vessel.

Because traffic on the old passenger routes was dropping with little prospect for improvement, the company concentrated on expanding its cargo-ship division. Since 1946, the airlines had gained the major share of passenger travel to Prince Rupert, Stewart, the Queen Charlotte Islands, and the main long-distance ports. Only the smaller and more isolated places depended on the year-round service of the Union ships. Still, passenger space on the new northern vessels was filled to near capacity in the summer by tourists.

In August 1950, a sister freighter to the Union's *Chilkoot II* was purchased from the Atlantic coast's sealing fleet, and steamed round to the Pacific coast, where she was commissioned as the *Cassiar III.* Three months later the old *Southholm* was converted to a barge and renamed the *Bulk Carrier No. 1.* A small tanker, originally named *Argo* but now the *Argus,* which carried 800 tons of liquid fuel, was bought for the Union-Waterhouse division. This was followed over the next two years by the hulking of two retired Canadian Pacific ships, the *Princess Mary* and the *Princess Maquinna,* which became *Bulk Carrier No. 2* and the barge *Taku* respectively. A military landing ship was obtained from Stockton, California, and turned into *Bulk Carrier No. 3.* The bulk carriers were operated in a barge pool under a joint arrangement with the Canadian Pacific employing the tugs and equipment of Straits

Towing & Salvage Company. The *Veta C,* another cargo-carrying tug with a capacity of 450 tons, was bought in 1952 and later renamed the *Chelan.*

The *Cassiar* and the Canadian Pacific's *Yukon Princess* under a joint contract carried south from Alaska the United Keno Hill mine concentrates until the White Pass & Yukon's own vessel was completed in 1955. The bulk carriers were engaged in transporting ore from Cominco's Tulsequah mine via Taku Inlet, Alaska, as well as ore from the Portland Canal mines and the Britannia mine in Howe Sound.

Union-Waterhouse vessels now encountered competition on several cargo routes from ships of the Northland Navigation Co. Ltd., whose managing head was Capt. Harry C. Terry, a former dock superintendent from the Frank Waterhouse Company.

Another fine little freighter, the 195.0′ *City of Belleville* with a capacity of 500 tons, was brought to Vancouver from the Great Lakes in October 1951. She was converted to a diesel motor vessel and renamed the *Capilano III.* The *Gulf Mariner,* an old south-coast competitor in 1947 and owned by Gulf Lines Ltd., had been converted for a second time to a tug, with a 300-ton freight capacity, and was under charter to Union-Waterhouse jointly with Straits Towing in 1952. The Union-Waterhouse division now had six freighters and a tanker in operation, besides several tugs owned or chartered and the four bulk carriers.

Sparking the Union's post-war cargo boom was the mammoth Alcan project, started in 1949, for a town and aluminum smelter at Kitimat. It involved the building of the Kenney dam to divert a waterflow westward through a 10-mile tunnel into the Kemano Valley, and a gigantic underground powerhouse at Kemano Bay. Waterhouse ships carried machinery, vehicles, steel, and supplies for the Morrison-Knudsen contractors. The Union began passenger service to the new Kemano dock in November 1951. A series of charter trips by the Union's new *Coquitlam* and *Chilcotin* ferried thousands of construction workers to the Kemano bunkhouses. As soon as a dock was ready, a scheduled service began to Kitimat. Every week until 1954 the *Cassiar* or the *Island King* left Vancouver full of building materials, lumber, and huge vehicles for Kemano and Kitimat. But in the later stages of this project, the airlines cut heavily into passenger travel, capturing nearly all business.

Carl Halterman, who had been responsible for developing much of this cargo-ship expansion, died in May 1953. Another blow struck on 15 June when a disastrous fire gutted the *Argus* while she was taking on liquid fuel at the Ioco wharf near Port Moody, seriously injuring four seamen. Only the heroism of Capt. W. (Billy) Boyce saved the town from a catastrophe when he boarded his burning ship and cast a line to the tug *Sea Chief,* steering the *Argus* into mid-stream. Then he shouted "cut the tow" so that he could beach the *Argus* out of danger before jumping clear.

Less than a year later, on 16 April 1954, the *Chelan,* loaded with concentrates from Skagway with *Bulk Carrier No. 2* in tow, was driven off course in a gale onto a submerged reef. She went down with her tow at the entrance of Sumner Strait, west of Wrangell, with her crew of 14, including Capt. Cecil Roberts and 5 officers and engineers.

Important changes in the company's direction took place in 1954 when the Canadian Pacific Railway sold its controlling shares in the Union to a group headed by Senator S.S. McKeen, who became the president and chairman. Gordon Farrell, Union's president since 1943, withdrew from the board, his departure being followed at the end of June by Gerald McBean's retirement as managing director. McBean had served the Union line well, but was suffering from the strain of the company's post-war problems. He did not long survive his move to a partnership in Canada Shipping Company.

McBean was succeeded by Philip B. Cooke, a shipping executive of wide Pacific coast experience and a former manager of the Union S.S. Company of New Zealand, who came out of retirement to direct the Union's operations for the rest of 1954. He cut services and, after R.L. Solloway of Union-Waterhouse retired, combined the cargo and passenger sections again, restoring the entire fleet to one operation under the Union flag. Cooke also obtained the small freighter *Northern Express,* which was renamed the *Chenega,* and later put in diesel engines. John F. Ellis was appointed general manager on 1 January 1955, and I was made assistant manager.

A remarkable project was begun in late April 1955 to install diesel engines in the *Cassiar* alongside the Union wharf, under the supervision of Thomas W. Morgan, the company's superintendent engineer. The conversion work had to be done quickly because the vessel was due to be chartered a month later by the Department of Transport to deliver a full load of fuel oil in barrels and other urgent supplies totalling 1,200 tons to Tuktoyaktuk. The work was completed in the fast time of 85 days, and the *Cassiar* sailed on her Arctic voyage on 27 July under the Hudson's Bay Company's Capt. F.L. Coe, with picked Union officers and crew of 25, as well as Surgeon-Commander W.M. Greer who was on loan from the Department of Indian Affairs. It was almost the last sailing date that would permit her to complete her mission and return before the ice field closed in.

The *Cassiar* performed magnificently, with the Union's C.C. Wilson, L. Thompson, and Glenn C. Hunter sharing the watches, but because of ice conditions and poor charts she grounded four times, suffering serious hull damage and the loss of a swamped lifeboat, before arriving and unloading the main cargo in Cambridge Bay. The lateness of the season and the damage forced cancellation of the last leg to Tuktoyaktuk. On the homeward voyage she narrowly escaped being trapped in the ice pack, but reached Vancouver on schedule and underwent hull repairs that cost more than $100,000.

The *Cassiar* was indeed fortunate, since she was held stationary in ice for nearly 10 days during this trip. Glenn Hunter, who later became a marine surveyor, recalled that it was touch-and-go whether the ship could make it to home port because the ice was drifting south early. By chance, he had become acquainted with a fellow Scot aboard an American convoy that was using frogmen to update their Alaskan coast survey, and was warned by him of the dangers of certain areas the *Cassiar* would have to traverse on the return voyage. Hunter later recounted:

> This was invaluable data enabling us to steer clear of further strandings. One night during my watch I'll never forget. Suddenly I became conscious of an eerie coolness—beyond any ordinary cold in the atmospheric "envelope" surrounding the vessel—and I immediately rang down the engines. Daylight found us enshrouded on three sides in an ice lagoon that might well have crushed the vessel if we had not, with slow progress, retraced part of our course. Through it all, morale remained high and the spirit of the men was excellent. Commander Greer, the doctor, was a tower of strength on several occasions. One thing, though, everyone aboard, even the hardiest seamen, got seasick in the Gulf of Alaska storms during the last days of the voyage.

Prospects seemed promising for the more closely knit Union fleet in 1955, and wage demands of the Seamen's International Union appeared within reach of a settlement in early June. Negotiations dragged on, however, and suddenly the S.I.U. presented to General Manager Jack Ellis new conditions that were impossible to accept within the 24-hours' notice that were given. All the Union's regular sailings were halted by a strike on 3 July. The fleet was tied up until 10 September, with a loss of nearly $1 million in seasonal gross earnings. A costly settlement, imposing higher expenses, was a severe setback to the promising recovery and forced more service curtailments. The *Lady Cynthia,* the last of the day steamers, never resumed operation on Howe Sound. The small M.V. *Hollyburn* was chartered for PGE railway connections between Vancouver and Squamish until the rail line between Squamish and North Vancouver was completed in 1956.

The structure of the Union line was again radically changed in April 1956 when its parent company, Union Steamship Co. of B.C. Ltd., by then a holding company, was wound up and shareholders relinquished their shares for common and preferred shares in Union Steamships Limited. This weakened the reserve strength of the line, which had negotiated a $2 million bank loan after the strike.

On 11 September 1956, the Union bought the Tidewater Shipping Company with its three small motor vessels—the *Tournament,* the *Troubadour* (the former *Gulf-Wing*), and the *Triggerfish.* Tidewater's president, Capt. J.A. Macdonell, was brought in as executive vice-president after the merger.

Captain Macdonell streamlined the schedules to give faster service to the main ports, and instituted a new system of shipping containerized freight to many coastal points, having 1,000 plywood containers built. Then he bought the 125.0' M.V. *Redonda,* a roll-on/roll-off landing ship.

The cancellation of large picnics and public excursions, with the withdrawal from service of the *Lady Alexandra* after 1953, foreshadowed a major change in both steamer and ferry services to Bowen Island. The climax came with the development in 1956 of Evergreen Park resort, which changed the Bowen estate from a popular playground to a prestigious all-year continental-type resort. The famous old Bowen Inn was transformed into Evergreen Park Lodge, a superior hostelry catering to company and association conventions, as well as to visitors and sportsmen and featuring a sea-view dining room. A smaller area adjacent to the Snug Cove wharf still provided facilities for picnics.

Increased residential building brought increasing car-ferry demands. This led to the end of Tommy White's popular Sannie Ferries service, which he and his wife maintained for over 35 years without a serious mishap in the carrying of 1,500,000 passengers. On 7 December 1956, the American Black Ball line's *Bainbridge,* a passenger-car ferry, took over the Horseshoe Bay–Bowen crossing until the newly established provincial ferry system absorbed the B.C. operations of the Black Ball line.

In 1957, with reduced passenger demand, only one weekly northern sailing of the *Camosun* was scheduled to Prince Rupert. On alternate weeks she sailed from there either north to the Nass River and Stewart or across Hecate Strait into Masset Inlet and Port Clements. Every other week a cargo ship with minimum passenger space was sent to Cumshewa and Skidegate inlets. The other two converted corvettes were assigned to Alaskan cruises.

Captain Macdonell became president of the Union company in July 1957, with Senator Stanley McKeen retaining chairmanship of the board.

The summer of 1957 was a busy period for the Union's tourist ships. The *Chilcotin* was booked to capacity on all cruises to Skagway and Glacier Bay. The *Coquitlam*'s space was reserved for the season by Charles B. West, the Seattle operator of Arctic Alaska Tours. Intermediate routes were served by the *Cardena* to Butedale, and by the *Catala* to Port Hardy, Rivers Inlet, and Bella Coola. The trips were publicized as "freight-boat cruises" and the slogan caught on with the public. These were the informal and intimate kinds of easygoing coast trips that only the Union seemed able to offer. The four diesel freighters—*Cassiar, Chilliwack, Capilano,* and *Chenega*—carried profitable loads in season. The steam freighter *Chilkoot* was sold to Mexican buyers after the west coast pulp contract ended in April.

Despite the seasonal profit, over the year the company suffered a serious loss because of constantly rising operating costs. The federal subsidy, which was granted in November 1957 for the preceding year, was only $325,000, and President Macdonell stated that it would barely cover half of the deficit in serving the contracted routes and ports. Northland's competition had also drained off considerable cargo revenue, especially in the off-season months at Kitimat and Prince Rupert.

Further negotiations with Ottawa failed to obtain any adjustment of the 1957 loss, or any assurance of a further subsidy the next year. It came as a complete surprise, however, when President Macdonell told the senior staff that he was advising the government that the company was withdrawing from further northern passenger service as of

1 January 1958. The public announcement was equally shocking to Vancouverites and the residents of coast communities, especially those in the more isolated places whose livelihood depended so much on the Union's passenger ships. Protests came from all sources, but the federal government declined to intervene; yet it soon arranged, as a temporary measure, for the Canadian Pacific's northern ship to make additional calls with a special subsidy of $190,000.

Before the end of January 1958, President Macdonell informed Ottawa of the Union's intention to restore the *Catala* to service on her old route to Bella Coola via intermediate ports after reconditioning her and making alterations including a cafeteria for all meals.

The abandonment of the route was a cardinal error, for holding on to such a key route would have strengthened the renegotiation of the whole subsidy contract. It was most unfortunate that the value of subsidized service was itself seen as a major issue in the crisis. The company's need for postal subsidy had been clearly stated in its prospectus of 1889. Without such government assistance, no company could possibly survive making year-round calls with mail, passengers, and essential supplies to settlements on the islands and in the far-flung inlets of the B.C. coast. Progressive settlement of the coastal areas had been a primary objective of the Canadian immigration department in insisting on subsidy for the Union line.

The *Catala* resumed service on 21 April under Capt. Ernest Sheppard and received a hearty welcome from all ports on the Bella Coola schedule. President Macdonell in the ensuing months sought an annual federal subsidy of $150,000 for this particular route, and later in the summer sent a formal submission to Ottawa to reopen negotiations, indicating his plan to install diesel engines in the *Cardena* for this service when agreement was reached. A telegram of acceptance dated 8 August was received from the chairman of the Canadian Maritime Commission. A telegram dated 11 August from the same source cancelling the previous advice arrived after the same weekend. I heard later that the Northland line, with whom the government was apparently negotiating a northern contract, had agreed to have their newly acquired passenger vessel call at Bella Coola.

Capt. Harry Terry, Northland's president and the Union's freight competitor, had meanwhile taken advantage of a CPR coastal fleet strike in July 1958 to announce on 2 August the purchase of two of their passenger ships—the CP's *Princess Norah* (renamed the *Queen of the North*) and the small *Princess of Alberni*—thus qualifying for subsidy consideration. Soon afterwards, Northland Navigation Company was awarded the entire northern coast contract, which the Union's new management had so rashly surrendered on 31 December 1957.

After losing their subsidy, the Union's cargo ships met stiffer competition from the now entrenched Northland line. The long-term outlook for the Union was not encouraging. The company's fleet had already been depleted by the sale of three passenger ships, all three converted corvettes having been sold before the summer. The *Chilcotin* went to the Sun Line of Monrovia in February, and sailed as the *Capri* to Teneriffe. Before the cruise season opened, both the *Coquitlam* and the *Camosun* (whose name had been changed to *Chilcotin* to retain goodwill) were sold to Charles B. West's Alaska Cruise Lines. Renamed the *Glacier Queen* and the *Yukon Star* respectively, they remained for another season under the Union's management. These ships continued to sail out of Vancouver for many years under their veteran Union masters, Capt. Ernest M. Sheppard and Capt. William McCombe.

It became evident before the end of 1958 that there was no future for a second major line in the general coast service. Thus it was a shocked and saddened public who learned on 14 January 1959 that the remaining unsold vessels of the proud Union fleet had been sold to Northland Navigation Company. Those still in active service were the *Catala, Cassiar III, Capilano III,* and *Chenega.* The *Cardena* already had been laid up.

The decline and ultimate end of the Union Steamship Company undoubtedly were hastened by management's failure to secure greater tonnage in the decade preceding World War II, and by its almost panic post-war haste to carry out the uneconomical conversion of war-surplus vessels. Had these mistakes not been made, modern Union ships might still be plying many of the routes that the red-and-black-funnelled vessels pioneered and served for 70 years.

Recollections of the Union's friendly operation continue to fascinate both past and present generations. Behind these echoes of the once-familiar Union whistle lies an unconditional acceptance of duty that would be hard to comprehend in today's world of commerce. Indeed, the dedication that pervaded all ranks of the Union line might be difficult to achieve in other circumstances or in other times. It remains a cherished heritage of the coast people whom the Union ships and men had served in 200 isolated settlements and waypoints.

As Vancouver's own steamship line from its founding days, the Union Steamship Company formed an integral part of the city's mercantile growth while performing an equally vital role in the development of British Columbia's resource-rich coast. It is left for the professional historians to assess the economic value of the fleet in linking the pioneer coastal communities and thus fostering the early logging, fishing, mining, and tourism industries.

One thing is certain: the Union Steamship Company set a marvellous safety record in not losing one passenger during its last 45 years. Considering the great distance traversed by Union ships along British Columbia's rugged coast (seldom less than 25,000 miles monthly) and the volume of passengers carried (more than 250,000 in peak months), it is indeed an amazing record. It stands as a proud chapter in Canadian marine history alongside the illustrious chronicles of the world's great coastal fleets.

The Union Fleet in Photographs

ARGO
CAMOSUN II
CAMOSUN III
CAPILANO III
CASSIAR II
CASSIAR III
CHELAN
CHENEGA
CHILCOTIN
CHILKOOT II
COQUITLAM II
ISLAND KING & CHILLIWACK III
REDONDA
TOURNAMENT
TRIGGERFISH
TROUBADOUR

1 *Gordon Farrell, president and chairman of the board, 1943 to 1954; a director from 1929.*

2 *Gerald McBean, general manager, 1945 to 1946; managing director, 1947 to 1954.*

1

2

3 *The* Camosun II, *camouflaged in grey and armed, on war service to the Queen Charlottes.*

4 *The* Camosun II *performed invaluable wartime service to the Queen Charlotte Islands, serving the lumber camps and transporting air force personnel and supplies to the Alliford Bay air base.*

5 *The* Cassiar II *in Prince Rupert harbour as the S.S.* Prince John.

6 *The* Cassiar II *made extra wartime trips from Prince Rupert to the Cumshewa camps and the lumber and cannery plants in Masset Inlet, QCI.*

3

4

5

6

7 *Air photo of the* Island King, *renamed*
Chilliwack III, *with outbound cargo.*

8 *The trim* Chilliwack III *returning
from Port Alice with a load of pulp.*

7

8

9 *The* Chilkoot II, *a China-coaster type of cargo vessel, sailing from Vancouver on the Port Alice route, in command of Capt. D.A. Connell.*

9

10 *The* Chilkoot II *en route to Port Alice.*

11 *The* Chilkoot II *in Quatsino Sound,
   1947.*

10

11

12 *The* Coquitlam II, *first of the converted corvettes, newly painted white, passing the West Vancouver shore.*

13 *The* Coquitlam II, *with black hull, on northern B.C. route to the Queen Charlottes via the Inside Passage. She carried thousands of workers into Kemano and Kitimat in 1951–52.*

12

13

14 *Announcement of the* Camosun's
*weekly Prince Rupert and Alaska
service in 1946.*

111

UNION STEAMSHIPS LIMITED

Announcing

UNION STEAMSHIPS

NEW DIRECT SERVICE

To.. **PRINCE RUPERT AND KETCHIKAN**

Via Ocean Falls

In Effect Wednesday, November 20, 1946

UNTIL FURTHER NOTICE
[Supplement to Current Sailing Guide No. 128]

STEAMER "CAMOSUN" ★

Leaves Union Pier Every Wednesday at 9.00 p.m.

on WEEKLY SCHEDULE as follows:

NORTHBOUND (READ DOWN)		PORTS OF CALL PACIFIC STANDARD TIME			SOUTHBOUND (READ UP)
9.00 p.m. Wed.	Lv.		Vancouver	Ar.	3.30 p.m. Mon.
9.00 p.m. Thur.	Ar.		Ocean Falls	Lv.	3.30 p.m. Sun.
10.00 p.m. Thur.	Lv.		Ocean Falls	Ar.	2.30 p.m. Sun.
3.00 p.m. Fri.	Ar.		Prince Rupert	Lv.	11.15 p.m. Sat.
12.00 Mdt. Fri.	Lv.		Prince Rupert	Ar.	7.30 p.m. Sat.
9.00 a.m. Sat.	Ar.		Ketchikan	Lv.	11.30 a.m. Sat.
			(Alaska)		

☆ Equipped with Radar, Echo Sounder and Air-conditioning throughout.

The times of arrival and departure will be followed as closely as possible, but are subject to tidal and weather conditions.

Information and Tickets:

UNION PIER, foot Carrall St., Vancouver. Phone PAcific 3411   CITY TICKET OFFICE, 793 Granville St., Vancouver. MArine 5438
VANCOUVER, BRITISH COLUMBIA

Victoria Agency: 1 Belmont House, Phone Garden 7822   Prince Rupert Agency: F. J. Skinner, Third Ave., Phone 568

HEAD OFFICE:
Union Pier
Foot of Carrall St.
Vancouver
Canada

CARL HALTERMAN,
Vice-President.

G. McBEAN,
General Manager.

G. A. BUSHTON,
Traffic Manager.

UNION STEAMSHIPS

15 *The* Camosun III *outbound from Burrard Inlet to Prince Rupert and Stewart.*

16 *The* Camosun III, *converted and painted white, leaving Prince Rupert for Ketchikan, Alaska.*

15

16

17 *The* Chilcotin *cruising in spectacular Gardner Canal. Her Alaska cruises, organized by general passenger agent Harold N. Crompton, were booked to capacity for 10 seasons.*

18 *The* Chilcotin, *her hull painted black, performed relief service on the northern B.C. routes and was chartered to carry thousands of workers to Kemano and Kitimat in 1952 for the Alcan project.*

17

18

Ten Day Cruise .. S. S. Chilcotin

SAILING FROM UNION DOCK. VANCOUVER. B.C.

ACCOMMODATIONS ARE LUXURIOUS

RATES ARE REASONABLE

Rates include accommodation and all meals en route, but not aboard steamer while in port at Skagway

Per Person
Standard Rooms at   **$180.00**
All outside two-berth rooms, with fold-away beds. Hot and cold water. (Single rooms at $205.00 and $215.00).

Per Person
Upper Deck Rooms at   **$220.00**
All two-berth rooms with fold-away beds; private compartment containing toilet, shower (with tub bath $230.00).

Per Person
De Luxe Rooms at   **$255.00**
Large upper deck rooms with twin beds; private compartment containing toilet and shower.

RATES QUOTED ARE CANADIAN FUNDS.

Write

UNION STEAMSHIPS LIMITED

Head Office:
UNION PIER, FOOT OF CARRALL STREET
VANCOUVER, CANADA

Or See Your Travel Agent

Ketchikan, principal city of Southeastern Alaska

Cruising
10
PLEASURE-FILLED DAYS
ON BOARD S. S. CHILCOTIN

BRITISH COLUMBIA COAST
ALASKA
AND THE YUKON

CHILCOTIN

UNION STEAMSHIPS

UNION STEAMSHIPS

1951 SEASON   VANCOUVER CANADA

20 *The Chilcotin's deluxe*
accommodations featured in brochure
attracted special tour groups from all
over North America.

Sail to New Horizons
...THE LAND OF THE MIDNIGHT SUN

ENTRANCE LOBBY

MAIN LOUNGE

OBSERVATION ROOM

DINING SALON

CHILCOTIN

Your cruise ship, S.S. "Chilcotin" is modern, streamlined and completely air-conditioned throughout to provide every comfort and service for the traveller. She has an overall length of 252 feet, and her engines of 2750 H.P. are designed for a cruising speed of 15 knots. Navigation equipment includes radar, depth sounder and telemotor direct transmission steering gear. Interior accommodation features handsomely appointed public rooms. The main lounge is exquisitely furnished in modern tones for your every comfort and enjoyment. The carpet is removable for dancing on the hardwood floor. Here also are presented motion pictures and impromptu concerts. Forward on the promenade deck is the attractively appointed observation room. Panelled in light oak, the windows are all low-glassed to permit a panoramic view of the magnificent scenery enroute. The dining salon, elegantly decorated, seats sixty persons and is equipped to give de luxe service. The recreation boat-deck is planned for relaxation, games, diversions, all in the best traditions of shipboard.

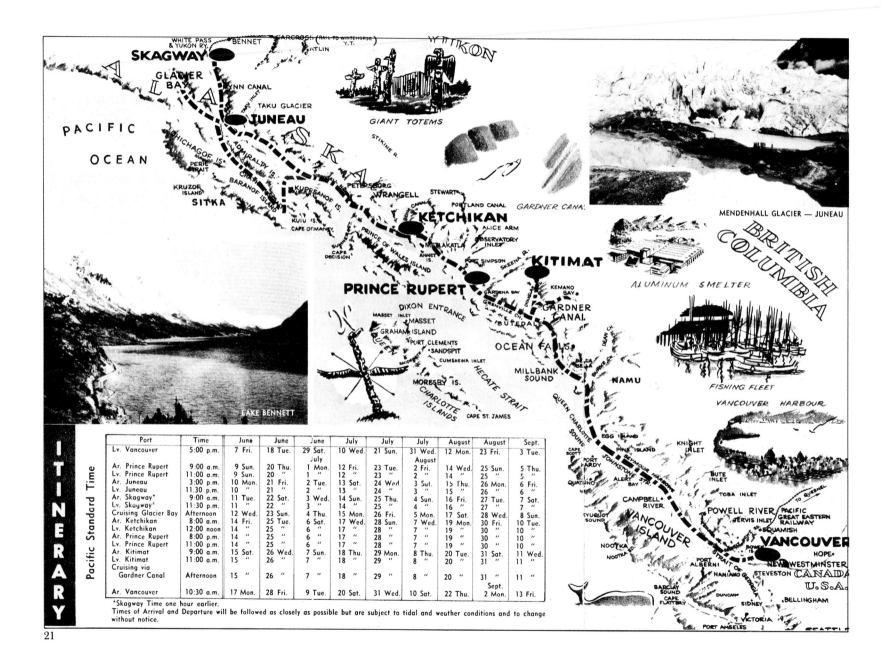

GIANT TOTEMS

MENDENHALL GLACIER — JUNEAU

LAKE BENNETT

BRITISH COLUMBIA

ALUMINUM SMELTER

FISHING FLEET

VANCOUVER HARBOUR

	Port	Time	June	June	June	July	July	July	August	August	Sept.
	Lv. Vancouver	5:00 p.m.	7 Fri.	18 Tue.	29 Sat.	10 Wed.	21 Sun.	31 Wed.	12 Mon.	23 Fri.	3 Tue.
					July			August			
	Ar. Prince Rupert	9:00 a.m.	9 Sun.	20 Thu.	1 Mon.	12 Fri.	23 Tue.	2 Fri.	14 Wed.	25 Sun.	5 Thu.
	Lv. Prince Rupert	11:00 a.m.	9 Sun.	20 "	1 "	12 "	23 "	2 "	14 "	25 "	5 "
	Ar. Juneau	3:00 p.m.	10 Mon.	21 Fri.	2 Tue.	13 Sat.	24 Wed.	3 Sat.	15 Thu.	26 Mon.	6 Fri.
	Lv. Juneau	11.30 p.m.	10 "	21 "	2 "	13 "	24 "	3 "	15 "	26 "	6 "
	Ar. Skagway*	9:00 a.m.	11 Tue.	22 Sat.	3 Wed.	14 Sun.	25 Thu.	4 Sun.	16 Fri.	27 Tue.	7 Sat.
	Lv. Skagway*	11:30 p.m.	11 "	22 "	3 "	14 "	25 "	4 "	16 "	27 "	7 "
	Cruising Glacier Bay	Afternoon	12 Wed.	23 Sun.	4 Thu.	15 Mon.	26 Fri.	5 Mon.	17 Sat.	28 Wed.	8 Sun.
	Ar. Ketchikan	8:00 a.m.	14 Fri.	25 Tue.	6 Sat.	17 Wed.	28 Sun.	7 Wed.	19 Mon.	30 Fri.	10 Tue.
	Lv. Ketchikan	12:00 noon	14 "	25 "	6 "	17 "	28 "	7 "	19 "	30 "	10 "
	Ar. Prince Rupert	8:00 p.m.	14 "	25 "	6 "	17 "	28 "	7 "	19 "	30 "	10 "
	Lv. Prince Rupert	11:00 p.m.	14 "	25 "	6 "	17 "	28 "	7 "	19 "	30 "	10 "
	Ar. Kitimat	9:00 a.m.	15 Sat.	26 Wed.	7 Sun.	18 Thu.	29 Mon.	8 Thu.	20 Tue.	31 Sat.	11 Wed.
	Lv. Kitimat	11:00 a.m.	15 "	26 "	7 "	18 "	29 "	8 "	20 "	31 "	11 "
	Cruising via										
	Gardner Canal	Afternoon	15 "	26 "	7 "	18 "	29 "	8 "	20 "	31 "	11 "
										Sept.	
	Ar. Vancouver	10:30 a.m.	17 Mon.	28 Fri.	9 Tue.	20 Sat.	31 Wed.	10 Sat.	22 Thu.	2 Mon.	13 Fri.

*Skagway Time one hour earlier.
Times of Arrival and Departure will be followed as closely as possible but are subject to tidal and weather conditions and to change without notice.

ITINERARY — Pacific Standard Time

CRUISES—North by West!

As well as "day outings", UNION offers a variety of longer cruises up to 10 days through the thrilling inland water ways and fjords of British Columbia.

6 DAYS—S.S. "CAMOSUN"
ROUTE 1, PRINCE RUPERT-STEWART — Leaves Vancouver every Wednesday 8 p.m. **RETURNS** about 8 p.m. following Tuesday. Upper deck with shower and toilet $123.25. Plus B.C. Tax, $1.32.

6 DAYS—S.S. "COQUITLAM"
ROUTE 2, PRINCE RUPERT-QUEEN CHARLOTTE ISLANDS — Leaves Vancouver every Monday 8 p.m. **RETURNS** about 8 p.m. following Sunday. Upper deck with shower and toilet, $116.75. Plus B.C. Tax, $1.23.

4 DAYS—S.S. "CARDENA"
ROUTE 5, MINSTREL ISLAND-RIVERS INLET. Leaves Vancouver every Tuesday 6 p.m. **RETURNS** following Saturday about noon. Main deck minimum rate $56.00. Upper deck with toilet $61.00. Main deck with tub-shower and toilet, $66.00. Plus B.C. Tax, 70c.

3½ DAYS—S.S. "CATALA"
ROUTE 3, OCEAN FALLS-BELLA COOLA. Leaves Vancouver every Saturday 8 p.m. **RETURNS** about 8 a.m. following Wednesday. $65.90 Minimum rate. Plus B.C. Tax, 82c.

2 DAYS—S.S. "CATALA"
ROUTE 3, ALERT BAY-PORT HARDY — Leaves Vancouver every Wednesday 8 p.m. **RETURNS** about 7 p.m. following Friday, $42.40. Minimum rate. Plus B.C. Tax, 53c.

All above times DAYLIGHT SAVING — APRIL 25 to SEPTEMBER 26.

As tourist accommodation is limited on several of the above routes, it is requested that enquirers give as many alternate dates of departure, trips, and types of accommodation acceptable, as possible.
This will assist in securing reservations. Rates are per person, quoted in Canadian Funds and include transportation and all meals and berth en route. All staterooms are outside and are for double occupancy. Most tourist space is on S.S. "Cardena", Route 5.

---
10 DAYS—S.S. "CHILCOTIN"
BRITISH COLUMBIA-ALASKA-YUKON. Exclusive cruise sailings every 10 days June thru September. Rates from $215.00 per person. Ask for descriptive folder.

RESERVATIONS

Out-of-town reservations may be made through leading Travel Agents or by writing direct to:—
H. N. CROMPTON, Passenger Traffic Manager,
UNION STEAMSHIPS LTD., VANCOUVER 4, B. C.

•

Vancouver Residents should apply to:

CITY TICKET OFFICE: 793 Granville St.   MArine 5430
or UNION PIER TICKET OFFICE   PAcific 3411

HEAD OFFICE

UNION STEAMSHIPS LIMITED

UNION PIER, FOOT CARRALL ST.
VANCOUVER 4, B.C., CANADA

Sunprinting   PRINTED IN CANADA

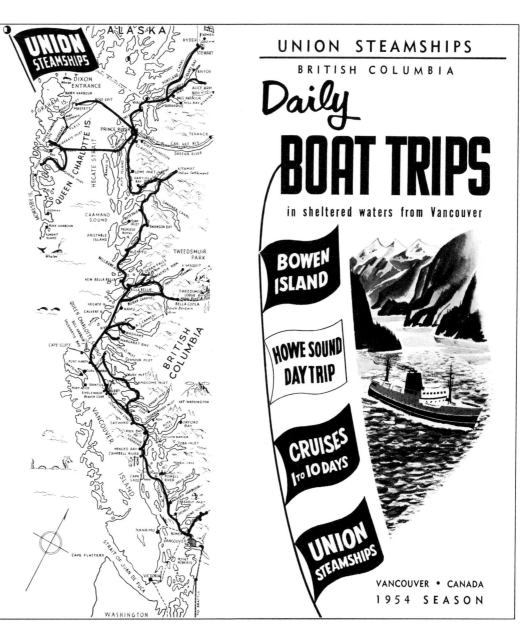

UNION STEAMSHIPS
BRITISH COLUMBIA
Daily
BOAT TRIPS
in sheltered waters from Vancouver

BOWEN ISLAND

HOWE SOUND DAY TRIP

CRUISES 1 to 10 DAYS

UNION STEAMSHIPS

VANCOUVER • CANADA
1954 SEASON

UNION STEAMSHIPS *Popular* ONE DAY TRIP

ALL-DAY HOWE SOUND CRUISE

Here's a real pocket edition of the Northern Fjords . . . an unrivalled short trip you can enjoy any day on "Vancouver's Glorious Inland Sea".

S.S. "Lady Cynthia" leaves Union Pier every morning for this scenic cruise through beautiful Howe Sound to Squamish, with interesting calls en route at Britannia and Woodfibre. This spectacular trip covers many place names of historic background.

BURRARD INLET—After Sir Harry Burrard, previously called Canal De Sasamat, by the Spaniards.

POINT ATKINSON—Famous lighthouse at entrance to Howe Sound, named after a friend of Captain Vancouver.

HOWE SOUND—After Admiral Lord Howe.

PASSAGE ISLAND—Named by Captain Vancouver, 1792 "in the middle of the Passage".

BOWEN ISLAND—Vancouver's Playground, named after Rear Admiral James Bowen.

QUEEN CHARLOTTE CHANNEL—After H.M.S Queen Charlotte, the flagship of Lord Howe.

HOOD POINT — After Admiral Sir Alexander Hood.

BRITANNIA — Site of one of the world's greatest copper properties — named from "Britannia Range" (H.M. S. Britannia fought tenth in line at Trafalgar.)

WOODFIBRE—One of Canada's leading pulp plants producing the highest grade of dissolving woodpulp in the world, largely used for rayon and plastics.

SQUAMISH—Southern terminal of the Pacific Great Eastern Railway, is a thriving little community at the gateway to Garibaldi Park. A former Indian settlement, it bears the name of the Squamish Tribes of the East Howe Sound region.

FULL DINING ROOM OR COFFEE BAR FACILITIES AT YOUR SERVICE ON BOARD

CRUISE FARE Mon. thru Fri. **$2.50**   SAT. & SUNDAY **$3.00**

Children 5 to 11 years half fare.

Leaves Union Pier 9:30 A.M. Returning 6:30 P.M.
All times Daylight Saving April 25 to September 26.

Howe Sound Cruise Map

Route of the DAILY CRUISE in beautiful HOWE SOUND

All steamers depart from **UNION PIER**, Foot of Carrall St.

Tickets and Information:
Up-Town Ticket Office
793 Granville St.
Telephone MArine 5438

Wharf Ticket Office
UNION DOCK
Telephone PAcific 3411

VANCOUVER CANADA

Spend a day at BOWEN ISLAND

BOWEN ISLAND

Visit "B. C.'s most popular seaside resort" at the entrance to Howe Sound where you can enjoy a splendid variety of things to do . . . or just laze on the sandy beach or in the lovely setting of Bowen Park.

There's popular recreation for everyone—swimming, boating, fishing, tennis, dance pavilion, sports grounds with complete facilities, cafeteria and hotel.

The excursion steamer leaves Union Pier every morning for this refreshing and scenic one hour's trip to Bowen Island . . . or you can make your visit via Horseshoe Bay (a scenic 12 mile drive by car or bus from Vancouver) where ferries connect hourly for the 20 minute trip from the Mainland to Snug Cove landing at Bowen Island.

Leave UNION PIER 9:30 a.m.
Leave BOWEN ISLAND 5:30 p.m.   **$1.55** Return

Children 5 to 11 Years Half Fare

Vacation at BOWEN INN

Its "Sea View" dining room welcomes both day visitors and vacation guests.

Enjoy a carefree holiday at BOWEN ISLAND INN set in a marine wonderland . . . relax at this companionable retreat with its colorful gardens. Meals are always appetizing with a wide choice of diversions, including reserved tennis courts, riding stables, lawn bowling green and a "Swim and Boat" float for Hotel Guests.

Accommodation in the Main Inn or in cozy bungalows alongside. Also Deluxe cottages with special features.

RATES (full particulars and folder on request) from $6.50 per day including meals. For reservations contact **City Ticket Office, 793 Granville St., Vancouver. MArine 5438.**

Day Trip to Bowen Island including Luncheon at Bowen Inn — **$2.90**

24 *The* Argo, *renamed the* Argus, *was obtained in 1950 to freight bulk liquid cargoes.*

25 *The* Argus *in Vancouver harbour.*

26 *The* Argus *approaching the Ioco wharf, the oil dock near Port Moody. She was destroyed there by fire on 15 June 1953. A major catastrophe was averted only by the heroism of Capt. W. Boyce.*

24

25

26

27 *The Union's largest and best cargo carrier,* **Cassiar III,** *in 1955.*

28 *With new diesel engines, the* **Cassiar III** *was chartered by the Department of Transport for an Arctic voyage and survived five strandings.*

27

28

29 *The* **Cassiar III** *easing her way through ice in the Beaufort Sea.*

30 *The* **Cassiar III** *close to shore in water almost clear of ice.*

31 *The* **Cassiar III** *discharging her cargo of petroleum products at Cambridge Bay, Victoria Island.*

32 *Local residents visit Capt. Frederick Coe on board the* **Cassiar III** *at Cambridge Bay.*

29

30

31

32

33: *The* Capilano III *approaching a
northern landing, her derricks and
slings prepared to discharge cargo.*

34 *The* Capilano III *proved a reliable
coastal freighter for intermediate
northern service to Prince Rupert.*

33

34

35 The Chelan, *shown as the motor vessel* Veta C.

36 The Chelan *was engaged in the Union-Waterhouse barge pool on towing contracts from Skagway, Alaska. She and her tow,* Bulk Carrier No. 2, *were lost in a gale off Cape Decision in 1954.*

35

36

37 *The Chenega as the steamer
Northern Express.*

38 *The 125.0' motor ship* Redonda *with
her roll-on/roll-off landing facilities
permitted heavy trucks to be driven onto
a beach anywhere. This facility plus her
liquid fuel tanks made her an ideal
vessel to serve the smaller off-channel
logging camps.*

39 *The* Chenega, *a small but useful and
economical freighter, after diesel engines
were installed.*

37

38

39

41 *The* Gulf-Wing, *a one-time competitor, was purchased and renamed the* Troubadour. *She gave fast passenger and small-freight service to local points and nearby logging camps.*

42 *The* Tournament III *as the* Jervis Express.

43 *The* Triggerfish, *shown in Vancouver harbour. This 100-ton freighter capsized off Whytecliff and was lost with three lives when her cargo shifted, 1956.*

42

43

44 Bulk Carrier No. 1, *the former*
Southholm.

45 *The* Princess Mary *before conversion to*
Bulk Carrier No. 2.

46 Bulk Carrier No. 2 *after "hulking."*

44

46

45

47 *The S.S.* Princess Maquinna *before conversion to a bulk carrier.*

48 *The* Princess Maquinna, *converted as the barge* Taku *in 1951.*

49 Bulk Carrier No. 3, *the former ARR 742 (landing ship), converted in 1950.*

47

48

49

50 *Thomas D. (Tommy) White, operator and owner of the Sannie Transportation Co. from 1921 to 1944, standing alongside his* Sannie IV. *The ferries made 30,000 crossings without a major mishap between Horsehoe Bay and Bowen Island. The Union company took over operation in 1944.*

51 *The* Sannie IV *ferry tying up at Bowen Island.*

52 *Sannie fleet at dock.*

53 *Horseshoe Bay-Bowen Island Sannie ferry fleet.*

50

51

52

53

54 *The ferry float landing alongside the main wharf in Snug Cove, Bowen Island.*

55 *Howe Sound ferries and water taxis.*

56 *The* Chilco, *a small Howe Sound ferry used in the Whytecliff service.*

57 *The* Chasina *of Howe Sound ferries which merged with the Sannie fleet after Whytecliff service was discontinued in 1951.*

54

55

56

57

Ships' Roster

☐ LEONORA

In Union service 1889–1904
Official No.: 80903
Type: Wooden tug. Built 1876 (hull at Moodyville) and completed at Victoria, B.C., by Joseph Spratt
Dimensions: Length 57.0', breadth 9.0', depth 5.3'. Gross tons 33
Engines: 15 NHP (high-pressure double engines, $7^{1/2}'' \times 8''$) supplied by Albion Iron Works, Victoria, B.C. Speed about 7 knots
Services: Moodyville ferry and Vancouver harbour towing
Capacities: Passenger licence unknown (about 25). Cargo 5 tons
General: Named for Louisa and Nora, daughters of Capt. James Van Bramer. Sold to Keefer's in 1904. Wrecked at Cracroft Island 1919

☐ SENATOR

In Union service 1889–1904
Official No.: 80902
Type: Wooden tug. Completed 1881 by Henry Maloney, Moodyville, B.C.
Dimensions: Length 51.5', breadth 12.0', depth 4.5'. Gross tons 31
Engines: Double engines $7^{1/4}'' \times 8''$ supplied by Albion Iron Works, Victoria, B.C. Speed 8 knots
Services: Regular Moodyville ferry to 1900 and local towing
Capacities: Passenger licence 30, cabin shelter for 12
General: Named for Senator Hugh Nelson, B.C. Lieutenant-Governor 1887–92. Later operated as a towboat by the Cates brothers, the Progressive Steamship Company, and Capt. Henrick (Harry) Grauer. After being taken off register, she was towed out and sunk in Manson's Deep off Bowen Island in 1925

☐ SKIDEGATE

In Union service 1889–97
Official No.: 72648
Type: Wooden tug. Built 1879 at Victoria, B.C., as a cannery tender and for towing. Rebuilt 1891 at Union wharf as a passenger-freight vessel passenger-freight vessel
Dimensions: Length 76.0', breadth 12.5', depth 6.0'. Gross tons 37 but altered in 1891
Engines: New Bow McLachlan engines (11'' and $22'' \times 14''$) in 1891, and speed increased from 9 to 11 knots
Capacities: Passenger licence originally 20 but increased after saloon built in 1891. Cargo capacity unknown but likely about 20 tons GM
General: Taken out of service in 1897 and broken up. Engines installed in *Chehalis*

☐ COMOX I

In Union service 1891–1919
Official No.: 100202
Type: Steel screw passenger-freighter. Hull prefabricated in sections by J. McArthur & Co., Glasgow. Launched from Union shipyard in Vancouver's Coal Harbour in 1891. Assembled by Henry Darling
Dimensions: Length 101.0', breadth 18.1', depth 5.2'. Gross tons 101
Engines: Bow McLachlan & Co., Paisley, Scotland. Compound 28 RHP. Speed 12 knots
Services: The first scheduled logging-camp vessel
Capacities: Passenger licence 200; 40 berths after being rebuilt in 1897. Cargo 100 tons
General: The first steel ship launched in B.C. (24 October 1891). Sold in 1919 to Vancouver Machinery Depot for break-up, but rebuilt as M.V. *Alejandro* for Mexican coast trade with diesels being installed

☐ CAPILANO I

In Union service 1891–1915
Official No.: 100203
Type: Steel screw freighter-passenger vessel. Hull prefabricated in sections by J. McArthur & Co., Glasgow. Launched from Union shipyard in Vancouver's Coal Harbour in 1891. Assembled by Henry Darling
Dimensions: Length 120.0', breadth 22.2', depth 9.6'. Gross tons 231
Engines: Bow McLachlan & Co., Paisley, Scotland. Compound 28 RHP. Speed 10 knots maximum, $8^{1/2}$ average
Capacities: Passenger licence 25 but increased in 1897 when berths added for Alaskan service. Cargo capacity 300 tons
General: The first British vessel to sail from a B.C. port in the Klondike Gold Rush 1897. Struck rock near Texada Island on 30 September 1915, and sank off Savary Island on 1 October

☐ COQUITLAM I

In Union service 1892–1923. Later as the Bervin *1939–50*
Official No.: 100205
Type: Steel screw freighter-passenger vessel. Hull prefabricated in sections by J. McArthur & Co., Glasgow. Launched from Union shipyard in Vancouver's Coal Harbour in 1892. Assembled by Henry Darling
Dimensions: Length 120.0', breadth 22.0', depth 9.6'. Gross tons 256
Engines: Bow McLachlan & Co., Paisley, Scotland. Compound 28 RHP. Speed 10 knots maximum, 9 average
Capacities: Passenger licence 24 (deck); rebuilt for Alaskan service in 1897 to provide 93 berths with licence 157. Cargo capacity 300 tons
General: Became the centre of an international issue when seized by American Customs 22 June 1892 in a sealing trade dispute (see main text). Sold to Bervin S.S. Co. in August 1923, and returned to Union fleet with Frank Waterhouse & Co. ships in 1939. Resold to Canadian Fishing Co. in 1950. Beached in 1959 at Malcolm Island as a breakwater

□ CUTCH

In Union service 1890–1900
Official No.: 88178
Type: Iron screw passenger-freight vessel. Built as a steam yacht in 1884 by J. Bremner & Co., Hull, England, for Indian potentate. Purchased by Union and steamed to Pacific coast in 1890 by Capt. W. Webster
Dimensions: Length 180.0', breadth 23.0', depth 11.7'. Gross tons 324
Engines: Compound 25" and 48" × 30". Speed 13 knots. Re-engined for Alaskan service 1898. Speed 14 knots
Services: Inaugurated regular Nanaimo service 3 July 1890. Vancouver-Skagway run from June 1898 to 1900
Capacities: Passenger licence 150. Accommodations rebuilt 1898 for licence 200 with 60 berths. Cargo 150 tons
General: Wrecked south of Juneau, Alaska, 24 August 1900 and abandoned to underwriters. Rebuilt 1901 as *Jessie Banning.* Converted to warship *Bogota* 1902 for Columbia in Peru conflict. Scrapped and sunk in South America

□ CASSIAR I

In Union service 1901–23
Official No.: 103472
Type: Wooden passenger-freight vessel. Built 1901 at Wallace Shipbuilding Co., False Creek, Vancouver, using hull of *J. R. McDonald,* a schooner launched at Ballard, Wash., in 1890
Dimensions: Length 120.6', breadth 29.0', depth 6.9'. Gross tons 597
Engines: Bow McLachlan direct-acting, inverted surface condensing, one multi-tubular boiler, single-ended amidships. Speed 9 knots. Coal burner, fuel consumption 17½ miles per ton
Services: B.C. logging-camp routes
Capacities: Passenger licence 144, cabin berths 42, also a loggers' saloon with open berths. Cargo 110 tons
General: One of the most colourful and famous ships to serve on the B.C. coast. Retired in 1923 and sold to Seattle interests in 1925. Ended her days as a floating dance hall on Lake Washington

□ CAMOSUN I

In Union service 1905–36
Official No.: 121204
Type: Steel passenger-freight vessel. Built 1905 by Bow McLachlan & Co., Paisley, Scotland
Dimensions: Length 192.7', breadth 35.2', depth 17.9'. Gross tons 1369
Engines: Triple-expansion 224 NHP; two boilers cylindrical multi-tubular. Speed 14 knots maximum
Services: The first large ship operated by the Union on regular service to Prince Rupert and northern B.C. ports
Capacities: Passenger licence 199, berths 68, deck accommodations 120. Cargo 300 tons
General: The first coastal vessel on the Pacific to have Marconi wireless installed in 1907. Retired in 1936 and later scrapped

□ CHEHALIS

In Union service 1897–1906
Official No.: 103065
Type: Wooden tug. Built 1897 by C. McAlpine, False Creek, Vancouver, B.C.
Dimensions: Length 59.7', breadth 13.3', depth 6.5'. Gross tons 54
Engines: Bow McLachlan (built in 1891) removed from the *Skidegate*
Services: Towing contracts and special charters
General: Chartered by Robert E. Bryce, and outbound was sunk in a collision in Vancouver's First Narrows on 12 July 1906, with loss of eight lives. An obelisk near Prospect Point in Stanley Park, with the victims' names, marks the location

□ COUTLI

In Union service 1904–9
Official No.: 116775
Type: Wooden tug. Built 1904 by George E. Cates, False Creek, Vancouver, B.C.
Dimensions: Length 71.4', breadth 18.8'. Gross tons 99
Engines: Compound. Bow McLachlan, Paisley, Scotland, 1903
Services: Towing contracts; used largely for B.C. Mills Timber & Trading Co.
General: The last Union tug. Sold in 1910 to the Red Fir Lumber Co., Nanaimo, after the Union withdrew from towing

□ COWICHAN

In Union service 1908–25
Official No.: 126210
Type: Steel passenger-freight vessel. Built 1908 by Ailsa Shipbuilding Co., Troon, Scotland. Launched as *Cariboo,* but name changed when registry duplication discovered after arrival on Pacific coast.
Dimensions: Length 156.1', breadth 32.0', depth 13.5'. Gross tons 961
Engines: Twin triple-expansion, 116 NHP, built by MacColl & Co. Two multi-tubular boilers, built by D. Rowan & Co. Speed 11 knots
Services: Union's main logging-camp routes
Capacities: Passenger licence 165, cabin berths 53. Cargo 125 tons
General: Sank in fog collision with *Lady Cynthia* 27 December 1925

☐ CHESLAKEE

In Union service 1910–13
Official No.: 130309
Type: Steel passenger-freight vessel. Built in 1910 by Dublin Dockyard Co. and completed at Belfast
Dimensions: Length 126.0', breadth 28.1', depth 10.0'. Gross tons 526
Engines: MacColl & Co., triple-expansion, 58 RHP. Speed 12 knots maximum
Services: Coast logging-camp routes
Capacities: Passenger licence 148, cabin berths 56. Cargo 120 tons
General: Sank at Van Anda wharf, after listing in storm, on 7 January 1913. Rebuilt and lengthened by 20 feet. Renamed *Cheakamus* (see below)

☐ CHEAKAMUS

In Union service 1913–42
Official No.: 130309
Type: Steel passenger-freight vessel (see *Cheslakee* above)
Dimensions: Length 145.3', breadth 28.1', depth 10.7'. Gross tons 688
Engines: MacColl & Co., triple-expansion, 58 RHP. Speed 12 knots, 10½ average
Services: Main logging routes, latterly on local trips
Capacities: Passenger licence 148, berths 56. Cargo 120 tons
General: Converted into a towboat, and a hull purchased for use as a barge in 1942. Sold the same year to the U.S. Department of Transport for $75,000 as a salvage tug

☐ CHELOHSIN

In Union service 1911–49
Official No.: 130805
Type: Steel twin-screw passenger-freight vessel. Built 1911 at Dublin Dockyard Co., Ireland, and completed at Belfast
Dimensions: Length 175.5', breadth 35.1', depth 14.0'. Gross tons 1,134
Engines: Twin triple-expansion, IHP 1,420, MacColl & Co., Belfast. Two multi-tubular boilers amidships. Speed 14 knots maximum, 12½ average
Services: Operated at first to Prince Rupert on the main northern route and later on principal logging route and to Port Hardy
Capacities: Passenger licence 191, cabin berths 66, deck settees 95. Cargo 150 tons
General: One of the Union's all-time most popular ships. Ran aground outside Vancouver's harbour entrance near Siwash Rock 4 November 1949, and abandoned to underwriters. Later refloated but not operated again. Dismantled in 1951

☐ VADSO

In Union service 1911–14
Official No.: 124077
Type: Steel freighter and passenger vessel. Built 1881 at Motala, Sweden, as the *Bordeaux*. Purchased 1907 by Boscowitz Co. and brought from Liverpool to Pacific coast as the *Vadso*. Taken over by Union in September 1911
Dimensions: Length 191.2', breadth 28.7', depth 21.7'. Gross tons 908
Engines: Compound. Speed 11 knots
Services: Northern cannery trade
Capacities: Passenger licence 50. Cargo 400 tons
General: Carrying only cargo, was wrecked and burned near mouth of Nass River, with no loss of life, on 3 February 1914

☐ VENTURE

In Union service 1911–46
Official No.: 129475
Type: Steel twin-screw passenger-freight vessel. Built 1910 by Napier & Miller, Old Kilpatrick, Scotland, for Boscowitz Co. Taken over in September 1911 by Union
Dimensions: Length 180.4', breadth 32.0', depth 17.0'. Gross tons 1,011
Engines: Direct-acting, triple-expansion, IHP 1,150, built by Miller & Macfie. Speed 13 knots
Services: Built specifically for northern cannery trade, and continued on Skeena River route seasonally
Capacities: Passenger licence 186, cabin berths 60, deck settees 85. Cargo 550 tons. Equipped with Marconi wireless
General: A splendid sea-boat and popular northern ship. Sold to Chinese firm in 1946, renamed *Hsin Kong So*. Badly damaged by fire en route to Orient. Destroyed by fire at Hong Kong 1947

☐ MELMORE

In Union fleet 1914–16, but operated only in 1914
Official No.: 99833
Type: Steel twin-screw passenger-freight vessel. Built 1892 for the Earl of Leitrim and operated between Glasgow and Northern Ireland ports. Bought in 1905 by Great Western Railway for service between Weymouth and Channel Islands. Sold and brought to Vancouver in 1913. Bought in January 1914 by Union and converted for excursion trade
Dimensions: Length 156.0', breadth 26.0' depth 11.3'. Gross tons 424
Engines: Compound, 96 RHP. Speed (after reconditioning) 12 knots
Services: Excursions during summer of 1914 to Sechelt and Seaside Park, also on evening trips in Howe Sound and to Indian River up the north arm of Burrard Inlet
Capacities: Passenger licence (summer) 475. Cargo 50 tons
General: Laid up after Labour Day. Sold to Peru in 1916 as the *Santa Elena*

□ WASHINGTON

In Union service 1918 only
Official No.: Unavailable
Type: Steel passenger-freight vessel. Built 1914 at Dockton, Wash., by J.A. Martinolich
Dimensions: Length 125.5', breadth 25.8', depth 7.3'. Gross tons 306
Engines: Triple-expansion, NHP 51, built by Hutton, Seattle. Speed 12 knots
Services: Brief trial only for excursions on Sechelt route
Capacities: Passenger licence 350. Cargo about 50 tons
General: Hull resold after engines removed

□ CHASINA

In Union service 1917–23
Official No.: 85075
Type: Iron passenger-freight vessel. Built 1881 by J. Elder & Co., Glasgow, as steam yacht *Santa Cecilia* for the Marquis of Anglesea. Renamed *Selma* under new owners before arrival at Vancouver under Capt. Charles Polkinghorne in 1910, and bought by All-Red Line. Renamed *Chasina* when Union took over their service in 1917
Dimensions: Length 141.8', breadth 22.1', depth 11.6'. Gross tons 258
Engines: Compound 80 RHP. Speed 13½ knots maximum, 11½ average
Services: On Vancouver-Powell River route
Capacities: Passenger licence 200 (winter 153). Cargo 40 tons
General: As a yacht, the *Santa Cecilia* had King Edward VII and Lillie Langtry aboard among many other distinguished guests. Sold in 1923, being reported as a rum-runner. After resale in 1931, she left Hong Kong 6 September but was never heard from again—a mystery of the sea

□ CHILCO & LADY PAM

In Union service 1917–35 as the Chilco. *Renamed* Lady Pam, *continued in service 1935–46, with passenger accommodations rebuilt*
Official No.: 87034
Type: Steel passenger-freight vessel. Built 1883 by J. Elder & Co., Glasgow, as a clipper-bow steam yacht, *Santa Maria,* for John A. Rolls. Later owned by Lord Hartswell, and in 1914 was steamed to the Pacific coast after being purchased by All-Red Line. Renamed *Chilco* when taken over by Union
Dimensions: Length 151.0', breadth 22.0', depth 12.6'. Gross tons 305
Engines: Direct-acting, compound 80 RHP. Speed 13 knots, 11½ average
Services: On Vancouver-Powell River route as the *Chilco,* alternating with the *Chasina* for a period. The *Lady Pam* was employed generally in West Howe Sound, serving summer camps and local routes
Capacities: Passenger licence as the *Chilco* 200 (winter 144), but later, as the *Lady Pam,* 130 all year. Cargo 40 tons
General: After withdrawal, used as a breakwater at Oyster Bay near Comox

□ CHILLIWACK I

In Union service 1919–26
Official No.: 119063
Type: Steel freighter. Built 1903 by Scott & Co., Bowling, Scotland, as the *Onyx* and renamed *British Columbia* by Coastwise Tugboat & Barge Co. Bought by Union in January 1919 and renamed *Chilliwack*
Dimensions: Length 170.7', breadth 27.0', depth 12.9'. Gross tons 557
Engines: Triple-expansion, 81 NHP. Scotch marine boilers built by Ross & Duncan. Speed 9 knots
Services: Largely in cannery trade, and in carrying bulk ore
Capacities: Cargo 750 tons, 15,000 cases of salmon, 325 M ft. of lumber. Passenger licence 10, berths 4
General: Retired 1926, and sold to Gosse Packing Co. as a floating cannery

□ CHILKOOT I

In Union service 1920–34
Official No.: 141710
Type: Steel freighter. Built 1920 by Wallace Shipbuilding Co., North Vancouver. Designed by Henry Darling for northern trade
Dimensions: Length 172.6', breadth 30.2', depth 12.9'. Gross tons 756
Engines: Inverted vertical triple, IHP 725, from Builders Iron Foundry, Providence, U.S.A., Scotch marine boiler from Vulcan Iron Works, Vancouver. Speed 12 knots maximum
Capacities: Cargo 800 tons. Heavy derrick 20-ton, 20,000 cases of salmon, 400 M ft. of lumber. Passenger licence 12, cabin berths 2
General: Sold to Border Line 1934; later to B.C. Steamships (Northland) and dieselized as *Alaska Prince*

□ CAPILANO II

In Union service 1920–49
Official No.: 141709
Type: Wooden single-screw passenger and freight vessel. Built 1920 at B.C. Marine, Vancouver, B.C.
Dimensions: Length 135.0', breadth 26.9', depth 8.2'. Gross tons 374
Engines: Inverted direct-acting, triple-expansion, NHP 51, built in 1914 for the *Washington.* Speed 13½ knots maximum
Services: Operated first to Selma resort and gulf coast points, and later generally to Bowen Island and Howe Sound, with PGE Railway connections
Capacities: Passenger licence May to September 350 (winter 150). Cargo 50 tons
General: A buffet saloon replaced its dining room in 1946. Retired in 1949

☐ CHEAM

In Union service 1920–23
Official No.: 96995
Type: Wooden twin-screw passenger-freighter.
Built 1901 as the *City of Nanaimo* by McAlpine &
Allen at False Creek, Vancouver, B.C. Purchased
later by Capt. J.A. Cates and renamed *Bowena* for
Terminal Steam Navigation run to Bowen Island
and Howe Sound. Taken over by Union with the
Bowen resort in December 1920 and renamed
Cheam
Dimensions: Length 159.0', breadth 32.0',
depth 9.4'. Gross tons 821
Engines: Compound, NHP 51. Speed 10½ knots
Services: Continued on the Bowen Island
excursion run and on the Britannia-Squamish
route
Capacities: Passenger licence summer 500, winter
200. Cargo 200 tons
General: Retired 1923 and became a floating
bunkhouse. Scrapped 1926

☐ LADY EVELYN

In Union service 1923–36
Official No.: 109680
Type: Steel twin-screw passenger-freighter. Built
1901 as the *Deerhound* by J. Jones & Sons at
Birkenhead for the West Cornwall S.S. Co. Later
engaged on the St. Lawrence River mail run from
Rimouski, Quebec, as the *Lady Evelyn,* and in
rescue work after the *Empress of Ireland* disaster.
Bought by Union from Howe Sound Navigation
in 1923
Dimensions: Length 189.0', breadth 26.1',
depth 9.5'. Gross tons 588
Engines: Triple-expansion, NHP 150, IHP 1,500,
two engines. Speed 14 knots maximum,
13 average
Services: Generally on West Howe Sound and gulf
coast routes
Capacities: Passenger licence summer 480, winter
200. Cargo 100 tons
General: Laid up in 1936 at Bidwell Bay and
scrapped

☐ CARDENA

In Union service 1923–59
Official No.: 150977
Type: Steel twin-screw passenger and cargo
steamer. Built 1923 by Napier & Miller, Old
Kilpatrick, Scotland
Dimensions: Length 226.8', breadth 37.1',
depth 18.4'. Gross tons 1,559
Engines: Direct-acting, triple-expansion,
IHP 2,000. Speed 14 knots maximum, 13 average
Services: Weekly on northern cannery route to the
Skeena River, also in the Bella Coola and
logging-camp services
Capacities: Passenger licence 250, cabin berths
132, deck settees 60. Cargo 350 tons; refrigeration
for 30 tons boxed fish; carried 11,000 cases of
canned salmon
General: With the *Cardena*'s reputation as a fine
sea-boat, no more popular ship sailed under the
Union flag

☐ LADY ALEXANDRA

In Union service 1924–53
Official No.: 151207
Type: Steel twin-screw passenger and freight
vessel. Built 1924 by Coaster Construction Co.,
Montrose, Scotland
Dimensions: Length 225.4', breadth 40.1',
depth 9.7'. Gross tons 1,396
Engines: Reciprocating steam triple-expansion, two
engines NHP 270, IHP 2,000; Yarrow water-tube
boilers. Speed 14 knots
Services: To Bowen Island resort and on Howe
Sound to Squamish. Made twice-weekly evening
dance cruises, and a variety of public excursions
through the summer season
Capacities: Passenger licence 1,400 (Howe Sound);
1,200 on special excursions, 900 to Victoria or
Nanaimo. Six staterooms (12 berths). Dining
saloon seated 86, convertible for dancing with
band podium. Cargo 300 tons
General: The best-known excursion steamer north
of San Francisco, and regarded as Vancouver's
"Excursion Queen." After being laid up in 1954
she was sold and became a floating restaurant in

Coal Harbour. Later on Pacific coast was
renamed *Princess Louise II.* In March 1980 at
Redondo Beach she was scuttled after listing in a
severe storm

☐ CATALA

In Union service 1925–59
Official No.: 152822
Type: Steel twin-screw passenger-freighter. Built
1925 by Coaster Construction Co., Montrose,
Scotland
Dimensions: Length 218.0', breadth 37.1',
depth 18.4'. Gross tons 1,476
Engines: Triple-expansion, 200 NHP; Yarrow
water-tube boilers. Speed 14 knots
Services: Weekly on northern main route to Prince
Rupert and Stewart. Later in regular service to
Port Hardy and Bella Coola
Capacities: Passenger licence 267, cabin berths
120, deck 48. Cargo 300 tons; refrigeration for 30
tons of boxed fish
General: A fine cruise ship, with a circular
promenade deck. After being taken over in 1959
by Northland, she was bought by Nelson Bros.
Fisheries. Later used as hotel ship during Seattle's
Century 21 exposition, then moored at Gray's
Harbor and wrecked by a storm in 1965

☐ COMOX II

In Union service periodically between 1924 and 1943
Official No.: 152548
Type: Wooden passenger-freight motor vessel.
Built 1924 by Wallace Shipbuilding Co., North
Vancouver
Dimensions: Length 54.0', breadth 15.5',
depth 7.2'. Gross tons 54
Engines: Diesel Atlas Imperial, Oakland, Cal.,
3 cylinders, BHP 55. Speed 7 knots
Services: Used as a ferry between Whytecliff and
Snug Cove, Bowen Island, 1924–26, and again
1939–42, also for connections from Pender
Harbour to Jervis Inlet and Sechelt Inlet, as well
as charters
Capacities: Passenger licence 25. Cargo about 15
tons

☐ LADY CECILIA

In Union service 1925–51

Official No.: 152718

Type: Steel twin-screw passenger-freighter. Built 1919 as the minesweeper H.M.S. *Swindon* by Ardrossan Drydock Co., Scotland. Converted 1925 for the Union by Coaster Construction Co., Montrose, Scotland, as the *Lady Cecilia,* with upper deck added as well as sponsons for greater stability

Dimensions: Length 235.0′ (BP 219.5′), breadth 28.6′, depth 16.3′. Gross tons 944

Engines: Triple-expansion, NHP 250, IHP 1,600; Yarrow boilers. Speed 15½ maximum, 13½ average

Services: Employed on gulf coast and Howe Sound routes, and excursions

Capacities: Passenger licence summer 800 (excursions 900), winter 500; 3 staterooms. Cargo 75 tons

General: Retired in 1951 and sold to Coast Ferries

☐ LADY CYNTHIA

In Union service 1925–57

Official No.: 152899

Type: Steel twin-screw passenger-freighter. Built 1919 as the minesweeper H.M.S. *Barnstaple* at Ardrossan, Scotland. Converted in 1925 by the Coaster Construction Co., Montrose, Scotland, as the *Lady Cynthia,* with upper deck added as well as sponsons for greater stability

Dimensions: Length 235.0′ (BP 219.3′), breadth 28.6′, depth 16.3′. Gross tons 950

Engines: Triple-expansion, NHP 250, IHP 1,600; Yarrow boilers. Speed 15½ maximum, 13½ average

Services: Mainly on Bowen Island-Squamish route and excursions

Capacities: Passenger licence summer 800 (excursions 900), winter 500; 3 staterooms. Cargo 75 tons

General: Structural changes made in 1940, with aft funnel removed and observation room extended. Sold 1951 to Coast Ferries, and scrapped in Seattle 1957

☐ CHILLIWACK II

In Union service 1927–54

Official No.: 137049

Type: Steel screw freighter. Built 1917 as the *Ardgarvel* by Ferguson Bros., Port Glasgow, for carrying iron and trading off Britain, 20% above Lloyd's requirement. Bought by Union in 1927 and renamed *Chilliwack II.*

Dimensions: Length 200.3′, breadth 30.2′, depth 12.8′. Gross tons 834

Engines: Triple-expansion, NHP 90. Speed 10 knots

Capacities: Passenger licence 10, berths 4. Cargo capacity 1,100 tons. Heavy lift capacity 20 tons; packed 26,000 cases of salmon, and fitted with two fish oil tanks, 8,000 gal.

General: Sold in 1954 to the Micronesia Metal & Equipment Co., and renamed *Iron Shield*

☐ LADY ROSE

In Union service 1937–51

Official No.: 170429

Type: Steel passenger and cargo motor vessel. Built 1937 by A. & J. Inglis Ltd., Glasgow; launched as *Lady Sylvia.* Because of registry duplication, was renamed *Lady Rose* after arrival in Vancouver

Dimensions: Length 104.8′, breadth 21.2′, depth 14.3′. Gross tons 199

Engines: Diesel. One 220 BHP propelling unit and one 28 BHP auxiliary, supplied by National Gas & Oil Engine Co., England. Speed 11½ knots

Services: On West Howe Sound route. In 1940–41 she moved military personnel and supplies to Yorke Island fort, then was requisitioned by naval transport for west coast service 1942–46

Capacities: Passenger licence 130, winter 70. Cargo 25 tons

General: Sold to Harbour Navigation Co. in 1951

☐ NORTHHOLM

In Union service 1939–43

Official No.: 148183

Type: Steel freighter. Built 1924 by J. Towers Shipbuilding, Bristol, as the *Robert H. Merrick.* Taken over with Waterhouse Co. by Union in 1939

Dimensions: Length 150.2′, breadth 25.2′, depth 11.9′. Gross tons 447

Engines: Single, 81 RHP. Speed 10 knots

Capacities: Cargo 550 tons

General: Foundered in fierce gale off Cape Scott on 16 January 1943, with loss of 15 of 17 crewmen. She was carrying pulp from Port Alice

☐ EASTHOLM

In Union service 1939–57

Official No.: 134071

Type: Wooden freighter. Built 1913 by A. Moscrop, Vancouver, B.C., and taken over with Waterhouse Co. by Union with Waterhouse Co. in 1939

Dimensions: Length 93.0′, breadth 24.3′, depth 6.8′. Gross tons 174

Engines: Single, 16 NHP. Speed 8 knots

Services: Local cargo service and contracts

Capacities: Cargo 250 tons

☐ SOUTHHOLM

In Union service 1939–50

Official No.: 141544

Type: Steel freighter. Built 1919 by Canadian Car & Foundry, Fort William, Ont. as the *E. D. Kingsley.* Taken over with Waterhouse Co. by Union in 1939

Dimensions: Length 200.0′, breadth 32.0′, depth 14.5′. Gross tons 1,029

Engines: Single, 825 IHP. Speed 10 knots

Capacities: Cargo 1,100 tons

General: Converted in 1950 into barge *Bulk Carrier No. 1*

☐ GRAY

In Union service 1939–44
Official No.: 124395
Type: Steel freighter. Built 1909 by R. Williamson & Son, Workington, England, as the *Petriana.* Operated on B.C. coast in 1910 by Northern Steamships. On charter when taken over by Union from Waterhouse Co. but later purchased
Dimensions: Length 182.7', breadth 27.9', depth 12.3'. Gross tons 707
Engines: Single, 90 RHP. Speed (estimated) 9 knots
Capacities: Cargo 650 tons
General: Sold in 1946

☐ CAMOSUN II

In Union service 1940–45
Official No.: 124202
Type: Steel passenger-freight vessel. Built 1907 by Ailsa Shipbuilding Co., Ayr, Scotland, as the *St. Margaret* for the North of Scotland and Orkney & Shetland Navigation Co. Later operated as the *Chieftain.* Renamed *Prince Charles* on purchase by CN Steamships for the Queen Charlotte Islands service. Bought and renamed by the Union
Dimensions: Length 241.7', breadth 33.1', depth 11.1'. Gross tons 1,344
Engines: Single, triple-expansion, 257 NHP. Speed 13 knots
Services: In continuous wartime operation between Vancouver, the Queen Charlottes, and Prince Rupert
Capacities: Passenger licence on Queen Charlottes route, 150, otherwise 178; cabin berths 87. Cargo 150 tons
General: Sold in 1945 to Greek owners and renamed *Cairo*

☐ CASSIAR II

In Union service 1940–49
Official No.: 127472
Type: Steel passenger-freight vessel. Built 1910 by Scott & Sons, Bowling, Scotland, as the *Amethyst.* Bought 1911 by GTP Steamships and renamed *Prince John.* Purchased from Canadian National S.S. 1940
Dimensions: Length 185.3', breadth 29.6', depth 11.9'. Gross tons 905
Engines: Triple-expansion, 136 NHP, 850 IHP. Speed 11 knots
Services: Queen Charlotte Islands direct and via Prince Rupert in 1940–41; continued in cargo and general northern service
Capacities: Passenger licence 85, cabin berths 38. Cargo 400 tons
General: Retired 1949 and scrapped 1951 in San Francisco

☐ CHILKOOT II

In Union service 1946–57
Official No.: 176882
Type: Steel freighter, China-coaster type. Taken over by Union while building at Victoria Machinery Depot, Victoria, B.C., and completed 1946
Dimensions: Length 214.1', breadth 36.7', depth 19.9'. Gross tons 1,336
Engines: Single, triple-expansion IHP 900. Speed 11 knots
Services: Port Alice cargo and pulp route, for which she was completed, until 1956
Capacities: Passenger licence 4. Cargo 1,500 tons
General: The last of the Union's steam freighters, she was sold to Navieros Unidos Del Pacifico S. A., Mazatlan, Mexico, in 1957

☐ COQUITLAM II

In Union service 1946–58
Official No.: 176902
Type: Steel passenger-freight vessel (former Castle-class corvette). Built 1943 by Smith's Dock Co., Middlesbrough, England, as H.M.S. *Leaside.* Converted in 1946 by West Coast Shipbuilders Ltd., Vancouver, B.C.
Dimensions: Length 235.6', breadth 36.6', depth 22.2'. Gross tons 1,835
Engines: Triple-expansion, IHP 2,800. Speed 15 knots maximum
Services: Queen Charlotte Islands and northern B.C. routes, also Alaskan cruise service
Capacities: Passenger licence 200, berths 114, deck 24. Cargo 250 tons
General: Sold in 1958 to Alaska Cruise Lines and renamed *Glacier Queen*

☐ CAMOSUN III

In Union service 1946–58
Official No.: 176903
Type: Steel passenger-freight vessel (former Castle-class corvette). Built 1943 by Smith's Dock Co., Middlesbrough, England, as H.M.S. *St. Thomas.* Converted in 1946 by Burrard Dry Dock Co., North Vancouver, B.C.
Dimensions: Length 235.7', breadth 36.6', depth 22.2'. Gross tons 1,835
Engines: Triple-expansion, IHP 2,800. Speed 15 knots maximum
Services: Northern B.C. and Queen Charlotte Islands routes, and later several seasons in Alaskan cruise service
Capacities: Passenger licence 200, berths 114, deck 16. Cargo 250 tons
General: Name changed to *Chilcotin* after sale of that vessel February 1958. Sold in June the same year to Alaska Cruise Lines and renamed *Yukon Star*

☐ CHILCOTIN

In Union service 1947–58
Official No.: 178070
Type: Steel passenger-freight vessel (former Castle-class corvette). Built 1944 by Henry Robb Ltd., Leith, Scotland, as H.M.S. *Hespeler*
Dimensions: Length 235.7', breadth 36.6', depth 22.2'. Gross tons 1,837
Engines: Triple-expansion, IHP 2,800. Speed 15 knots
Services: Completed specifically for Alaskan summer cruises, with extra features for tourist entertainment. Used for winter relief service only on Union's northern routes
Capacities: Passenger licence 200, first-class berths 106; deck none. Cargo 250 tons
General: Sold to Sun Line, Monrovia, in February 1958 and renamed *Capri*. Later refitted for cruises from the St. Lawrence as *Stella Maris*. Bought by Seattle owners in 1965. Destroyed by fire at Sardinia

☐ ISLAND KING & CHILLIWACK III

In Union service 1944–54 as Island King. Renamed Chilliwack III, *continued in service 1954–59*
Official No.: 160634
Type: Steel cargo motor vessel. Built 1920 by Trosvik Mer. Verk at Brevik, Norway, as the *Granit* and later named *Columba*. Bought for Waterhouse operation in 1944 and renamed *Chilliwack* in 1954 to preserve that name in the fleet
Dimensions: Length 165.1', breadth 28.2', depth 12.4'. Gross tons 591
Engines: Diesel BHP 400. Speed 10 knots, increased as *Chilliwack III* to 11 knots
Services: On west coast Port Alice route, later in general service
Capacities: Passenger licence 4, increased to 12 in 1958. Cargo 800 tons
General: Renamed *Tahsis Prince* by Northland in 1959

☐ CAPILANO III

In Union service 1951–59
Official No.: 172234
Type: Steel cargo motor vessel. Built 1946 at Port Arthur Shipbuilding Co. as *Ottawa Mayferry,* and later named *City of Belleville.* Renamed *Capilano* and dieselized after Union purchase in 1951
Dimensions: Length 145.0', breadth 27.1', depth 8.0'. Gross tons 530
Engines: Diesel BHP 400. Speed 12 knots maximum
Capacities: Cargo 500 tons
General: Renamed *Haida Princess* by Northland in 1959

☐ ARGUS

In Union service 1950–53
Official No.: 192573
Type: Steel tanker motor vessel. Built 1944 by Kyle & Co. at Stockton, Cal., as *Y-30* for U.S. navy. Bought from Pacific Petroleum Co. as the *Argo* and renamed *Argus*
Dimensions: Length 157.3', breadth 27.2', depth (hold) 19.9'. Gross tons 517
Engines: Diesel-powered. Speed 10½ knots
Services: Carried liquid petroleum and dry cargo
Capacities: Cargo 800 tons. Tanks for 200 M gal. liquid fuel
General: Destroyed by fire loading at Ioco, B.C., on 15 June 1953. Straits Towing Company converted the beached hulk into a transport barge in 1954

☐ CASSIAR III

In Union service 1951–59
Official No.: 176563
Type: Steel cargo vessel. Built 1946 by Burrard Dry Dock Co., North Vancouver, B.C., as *Ottawa Page.* Sold to Job Bros., St. John's, Newfoundland, and renamed *Blue Peter II* as depot ship for sealing fleet. Bought by Union 1951
Dimensions: Length 214.1', breadth 36.7', depth 19.8'. Gross tons 1,377
Engines: Originally triple-expansion, IHP 900. Converted in 1955 to diesel engine built by National Supply Co., Springfield, Ohio. BHP 1,440. Speed 13 knots
Capacities: Passenger licence 4, increased in 1958. Cargo 1,500 tons
General: Chartered by Canadian Department of Transport to supply RCAF Arctic posts in 1955. Renamed by Northland as *Skeena Prince* 1959

☐ CHELAN

In Union service 1952–54
Official No.: 193774
Type: Steel tug and cargo motor vessel. Built 1944 by Northwestern Shipbuilding Co., Bellingham, Wash., for U.S. navy, and later named *Veta C.* Renamed *Chelan* after purchase by Union
Dimensions: Length 148.0', breadth 33.3', depth 15.6'. Gross tons 541
Engines: Diesel-powered. Speed 12 knots
Services: Used in barge pool for towing, and for carrying bulk concentrates
Capacities: Cargo 450 tons
General: Lost with crew of 14 off Cape Decision, Alaska, while towing *Bulk Carrier No. 2* from Skagway on 15 April 1954

☐ CHENEGA

In Union service 1954–59
Official No.: 190831
Type: Steel cargo motor vessel. Built 1916 by Anderson Steamboat Co., Seattle, as lighthouse tender *Rose.* Bought by Union in 1954 as the *Northern Express* from General Sea Transportation Ltd., then dieselized and renamed *Chenega*
Dimensions: Length 129.3', breadth 24.6', depth 11.0'. Gross tons 381
Engines: Powered in 1956 with twin GM diesels. Speed 12 knots
Services: Northern B.C. cargo routes
Capacities: Cargo 350 tons, including refrigeration space

☐ REDONDA

In Union service 1955–59
Official No.: 192462
Type: Steel diesel cargo tanker, landing-ship class. Built 1944 at Portland, Ore., as U.S.S. *YTC No. 501-52*
Dimensions: Length 125.0', breadth 23.6', depth 6.6'. Gross tons 185
Engines: Diesel-powered. Speed 7 knots
Services: Roll-on/roll-off type to supply logging camps and upcoast plants
Capacities: Cargo 225 tons. Equipped with tanks for 50 M gal. liquid fuel

☐ TROUBADOUR III

In Union-Tidewater service 1956–59
Official No.: 176497
Type: Steel diesel passenger vessel and packet freighter. Built 1944 as a Fairmile by Star Shipyard, New Westminster, B.C. Converted and named *Gulf-Wing* by Gulf Lines Ltd. 1946. Bought by Tidewater Co. 1952 and renamed *Troubadour*
Dimensions: Length 107.6', breadth 18.0', depth 6.0'. Gross tons 103
Engines: Two 320-HP V-diesels. Speed 15 knots originally, 12½ average
Capacities: Passenger licence 95. Cargo 25 tons, express 10 tons

☐ TOURNAMENT

In Union-Tidewater service 1956–59
Official No.: 178056
Type: Steel passenger and freight motor ship. Built 1942 at Annapolis Boatyard, City Island, New York, and named *Jervis Express* before purchase by Tidewater Co.
Dimensions: Length 108.0', breadth 18.4', depth 7.0'. Gross tons 149
Engines: Twin diesels. Speed 15 knots maximum, 13 average
Capacities: Passenger licence 101. Cargo 40 tons

☐ TRIGGERFISH

In Union-Tidewater service only in 1956
Official No.: 179598
Type: Steel cargo motor ship. Built by G. Hittebrant, Kingston, N.Y.
Dimensions: Length 108.0', breadth 18.4', depth 8.0'. Gross tons 149
Engines: Diesel-powered. Speed 10 knots
Services: Logging route
Capacities: Cargo 100 tons
General: Capsized and sank off Whytecliff on 6 October 1956, with loss of 3 crewmen, when cargo shifted

☐ BULK CARRIERS (Barges)

Commando, 1942–46

Bulk Carrier No. 1 (Southholm, hulked in 1950)

Bulk Carrier No. 2 (Princess Mary, hulked in 1950)

Bulk Carrier No. 3 (U.S.S. ARR 742 landing ship, hulked in 1950)

Bulk Carrier Taku (Princess Maquinna, hulked in 1951)

Ship Names of Indian and Spanish Derivation

Camosun   This was taken from the Indian name for the bay where the city of Victoria stands. The Indians called the original settlement Camosack or Camosun, meaning "a deep, narrow gorge" or "swift-running water." Three Union ships carried this name.

Capilano   This is the English translation of the Indian family name *Ky-Ap-Lan-Huh,* meaning "of a great chief" (Indian royalty). Chief George Capilano (baptized George after embracing Christianity) escorted Captain Vancouver into Burrard Inlet with 40 war canoes on 15 June 1792. Chief Joe Capilano was received by King Edward VII, and Chief Matthias Joe attended the coronation of Queen Elizabeth. Three vessels with this proud name flew the Union flag.

Cardena   This is one of two Spanish names (the other being Catala) given to early Union ships. It was taken from Cardena Bay on the south shore of Kennedy Island at the mouth of the Skeena River, which appropriately was in the centre of the fishing industry the *Cardena* was designed to serve. Cardena Bay was named after García Lopez de Cardenas, one of Coronado's captains (later an admiral) in his New Mexico expedition. Cardenas is said to have been the first white man to see the Grand Canyon.

Cariboo   The *Cowichan*'s original name derives from the name of a large plateau in central and eastern British Columbia. The word is a variant of "caribou," the Indian name by which the North American reindeer is commonly known.

Cassiar   This most famous of the Union fleet's names was borne by three ships. It is a corruption of the Indian word *casha* or *caska,* meaning "a creek." The district from which it is taken contains many streams and extends between the Coast Range and the Rocky Mountains, along and north of the Stikine River. The name Cassiar originated with the Caska Indians, a division of the Nahane people, and is said to have been corrupted from Caska by the French-Canadian explorer Thibert.

Catala   This Spanish name was taken from Catala Island at the entrance of Esperanza Inlet on the west coast of Vancouver Island. It commemorates the pioneer missionary work of Father Magin Catalá, who was revered as a holy man for his sanctity and prophetic powers. Father Catalá came north to the Spanish settlement of Santa Cruz de Nootka and spent the years 1793–94 with the Vancouver Island Indians in that area, returning to California in 1795.

Chasina   The Indian name, with which the *Selma* was rechristened in 1917, comes from Chasina Island in the Okis Hollow channel west of Maurelle Island; its meaning is unknown. The Okis Hollow passage, generally restricted to small craft, was used regularly by the Union's logging route ships to enter Johnstone Strait from the Surge Narrows area as an alternative to the main route through Seymour Narrows.

Cheakamus   This ship was named for the Cheakamus River and Cheakamus Canyon north of Howe Sound. It is believed that the original Indian name was Chehagamus, meaning "a fish trap." For the first 2 of her 32 years in the Union service she was called the *Cheslakee.* The name Cheakamus was later transferred to one of the Union's small ferries.

Cheam   The old *Bowena* was renamed *Cheam* in 1921. It was the name of an Indian village in the outlying Chilliwack district, denoting "a wild strawberry place." It was also given to Cheam Mountain, pronounced See-Am, meaning "The Chief."

Chehalis   The name was taken from the small city of Chehalis, on the banks of the Chehalis River in southwest Washington State. Its Indian meaning has been given as "shining sand."

Chelan   This Indian name was chosen for the *Veta C* after 1952. It was taken from 50-mile-long Chelan Lake in north central Washington. The name is also borne by a falls, a river, and a city in the Cascades Range. The meaning of the word is "deep water" and the Indian pronunciation is Tsill-Ane.

Chelohsin   According to the Reverend C.M. Tate, an Indian missionary, this famous ship name means "open to the mouth," i.e., having a navigable entrance. It was an appropriate one for this vessel, which at one time or another entered almost every port or channel on the northern B.C. coast.

Chenega   This name was taken from an old Indian village in northwestern Alaska. It is not a Chinook word, nor is it directly connected with the British Columbia coast. So far as can be ascertained, the native word means "the gathering" of a northern tribe.

Cheslakee   This was the name of a once-populous Indian community on the Nimpkish River, off Broughton Strait, visited by Captain Vancouver and recorded in his journal as "Cheslakee's village."

Chilco   (See also *Chilcotin.*) The word Chilco means "the path or waterway of the Chil" (or Cinl), known today as the Chilcotin River. The original name of the *Chilco,* which operated from 1917 to 1935, was *Santa Maria,* later changed to *Lady Pam.*

Chilkoot   This name is derived from the Chilkat (or Chilkoot) Indians, a tribe in the Yukon and Upper Nass River territories. The tribal name was given to the famous Chilkoot Pass and the river. The pass, sometimes called "the poor man's road," was the land route to the Klondike during the gold rush years, 1897 to 1899. Both the *Chilkoot I* and the *Chilkoot II* were cargo vessels.

Chilcotin   This word in Indian dialect is said to mean "the people of the Chil (or Cinl) waterway." The Chilcotin country, which lies east-west between the Fraser River and the Coast Range, is an undefined maze of mountains and valleys in central British Columbia traversed by the Chilcotin River, a tributary of the Fraser. To many old-timers, the name is "Chilly-Cootin."

Chilliwack   This name derived from an upriver dialect of Halkomelem, meaning "go into a backwater (in the delta)," the "hair" of the river—a reference to a shortcut one can take canoeing upriver via Hope Slough. An Indian tribe gave the name to the Chilliwack area of the Fraser Valley where the first white settlers arrived in 1862. Three Union cargo vessels carried this name.

Comox   This was the Indian name with which the first Union ship was christened on being launched from the pioneer Union Steamship Company's shipyard in Vancouver's Coal Harbour. It is an abbreviation of the name in the Euclataw tongue for the Comox district of Vancouver Island. The full name is Comuckthway, meaning "plenty" or "riches"—the district being noted for its abundance of berries and game.

Coquitlam   This is one of the few Indian names in the lower Fraser Valley perpetuated in contemporary place names: the municipalities of Coquitlam and Port Coquitlam, the Coquitlam River, and Mt. Coquitlam (5,793 feet). It means "a small red salmon"—a fish that once teemed in the Coquitlam River but is now extinct. The name comes from that of a Salish tribe in the locality of the north arm of the Fraser River who spoke the Cowichan dialect.

Cowichan   The word Cowichan derives from the Halkomelem word *Q(a)w-(a)can,* meaning "warm mountains" —an apparent reference to sheltered uplands at the head of the Cowichan River. The Cowichan tribe lived in the area of southeast Vancouver Island, hence the place name Cowichan Bay.

■ ■ ■

All the early ships of the Union Steamship fleet were given Indian or Spanish names beginning with the letter "C"; but starting with the *Lady Evelyn* in 1923 and ending with the *Lady Rose* in 1937, all new day steamers were given the "Lady" prefix.

Acknowledgements

Our deep appreciation goes to the following individuals and institutions who have been so generous with their visual materials.

C. Allan Anderson Collection, Vancouver Maritime Museum: jacket cover photo

Judge J.J. Anderson: 1889–1918, nos. 20, 24, 31–33; 1919–1939, nos. 5, 11, 29, 30, 53, 56, 60, 65; 1940–1959, no. 43

H.C. Barley Collection, Yukon Archives: 1889–1918, no. 10

Campbell River and District Museum: 1889–1918, nos. 25, 28, 41

Harold N. Crompton: 1940–1959, nos. 29–32

James Crookall Collection, Vancouver Maritime Museum: 1889–1918, nos. 29, 36, 44

Constance Darling and Mary Darling: 1889–1918, no. 1

Gray Family Collection, Vancouver Maritime Museum: 1889–1918, no. 15

Norman R. Hacking: 1889–1918, no. 17

Budge Jukes: 1940–1959, no. 41

William T. Marks: 1889–1918, nos. 43, 49, 50; 1919–1939, no. 54; 1940–1959, no. 46

Puget Sound Maritime Historical Society: 1940–1959, no. 38

Mrs. Harold S. Putnam: 1940–1959, no. 3

Capt. Henry (Harry) Rouch. 1919-1939, no. 26

John Tadych: 1919–1939, no. 49

Union Steamship Company Collection, Vancouver Maritime Museum: 1889–1918, nos. 18, 19, 48; 1919–1939, nos. 1, 48; 1940–1959, nos. 1, 2, 12, 15, 19–23, 48, 49

Vancouver City Archives: 1889–1918, nos. 2–4, 7, 9; 1919–1939, nos. 9, 55, 61

Vancouver Maritime Museum: 1889–1918, nos. 5, 6, 8, 11–14, 16, 21–23, 26, 27, 34, 35, 37–40, 42, 45–47; 1919–1939, nos. 2–4, 6–8, 10, 12–24, 27, 28, 31–47, 50–52, 62, 66; 1940–1959, nos.5–7, 9, 10, 13, 14, 16–18, 24–28, 35, 37, 40, 42, 44, 45, 47, 50–56, 62

Vancouver Public Library, Historic Photos Division: 1919–1939, no. 25; 1940–1959, no. 11

Vancouver Public Library, Northwest Room: 1889–1918, no. 30

World Ship Society, Vancouver, B.C., Branch: 1919–1939, nos. 57–59, 63, 64; 1940–1959, nos. 4, 8, 33, 34, 36, 39